*Jean Giraudoux, Surrealism,*
*and the German Romantic Ideal*

# Jean Giraudoux, Surrealism, and the German Romantic Ideal

*By*
LAURENCE LE SAGE

ILLINOIS STUDIES IN LANGUAGE AND LITERATURE: *Vol.* XXXVI, *No. 3*

THE UNIVERSITY OF ILLINOIS PRESS
URBANA, 1952

Entre les domaines secrets de chaque littérature, malgré la barrière des langues, il est des communications possibles, et des passages que l'on peut franchir au plus profond de la sensibilité européenne, à force d'amour et de patience.

MARCEL RAYMOND, *De Baudelaire au Surréalisme*

# *Foreword*

THESE STUDIES are intended to be of esthetic affinities. The German Romanticists, whose creative talent could never rival their great predecessors Goethe and Schiller, formulated nevertheless a literary and artistic doctrine which was to prescribe the general orientation of literature down to the present day. Literature in France in the twentieth century appears as a fulfillment and elaboration of the theories enunciated in Jena and Heidelberg a century earlier. And spokesmen for this new age—as rich in criticism and theory as the German Romantic—reiterate the teachings of the German masters.

I am not primarily concerned here with influences. Although some important direct contacts may be established between writers of the two groups, generally speaking, they are linked historically only by very slender and indirect threads. It is not my purpose to dwell upon the development of Romantic ideas in Germany or abroad, their affiliations and affinities with English, American, and other poetic theory, their penetration into France at the time of French Romanticism, especially in connection with Gérard de Nerval, their filtering through French Symbolism. Such ramifications throughout the nineteenth century would lead into too vast an historical survey. Of the enormous and complicated story of the Romantic movement in European literatures I am here concerned with just a small part: the reaffirmation and realization by twentieth-century French writers of the Romantic ideal of the German school. Even within these boundaries, however, I can hope to present only some general lines and tendencies, leaving much unsaid and unexplored.

Of the major French writers and schools of this century Jean Giraudoux and Surrealism strike me as excellent examples of fulfillment of the Romantic ideal. For this reason I propose to devote to each one a particular chapter and survey methodically their principal points of affinity with the Germans. But they are only typical of their times. In a third chapter I should like to bring in other modern voices to attest to the general acceptance of the German Romantic point of view among the contemporary writers of France.

# Contents

# CHAPTER ONE

# Jean Giraudoux
# and the German Romantic Authors

JEAN GIRAUDOUX's kinship with German Romanticism has not gone unperceived. In trying to describe or place his art, numerous critics and reviewers have alluded to possible German antecedents or kindred geniuses. Several short articles have been devoted exclusively to aspects of this relationship. René de Messières called attention to the characteristically German device of Romantic irony in Giraudoux's work [1] and Fernand Baldensperger pointed out in general terms that Giraudoux's fundamental esthetic is close to German Romanticism.[2] More recently, several other contributions are to be mentioned: a comparison of *Amphitryon 38* with Kleist's play based on the same legend [3] and my studies of Giraudoux's contacts with German literature.[4]

## GIRAUDOUX'S KNOWLEDGE OF GERMAN ROMANTICISM

We are not to deal with any fortuitous encounter, one of those curious but not uncommon phenomena where an artist in his own independent peregrination seems to have wandered into a familiar path. Nor can we dismiss Giraudoux's affinity with the Germans as merely an indirect influence filtering down through French Symbolism. We know that Giraudoux served a lengthy and formal apprenticeship as a student of German literature. This most significant early chapter in his career offers indisputable evidence of a close familiarity with those German masters who seem to relive in his own pages, and permits us to observe the interesting process of his artistic formation and orientation.

### His studies and travels

While a student at the Ecole Normale, Giraudoux encountered Professor Charles Andler, whose dynamic lectures on German Romanticism were introducing to a generation of entranced students an esthetic point of view radically opposed to con-

[1] René E. de Messières, "Le Rôle de l'ironie dans l'oeuvre de Giraudoux," *Romantic Review*, XXIX (1938), 373–83.

[2] Fernand Baldensperger, "L'Esthétique fondamentale de Jean Giraudoux," *French Review*, XVIII (1944), 2–10.

[3] J. J. Anstett, "Jean Giraudoux et H. von Kleist," *Les Langues modernes*, August–October, 1948, pp. 385–93.

[4] L. LeSage, "Jean Giraudoux, Hoffmann, and Le Dernier Rêve d'Edmond About," *Revue de littérature comparée*, January–March, 1950, pp. 103–7.

———, "Fouqués Undine, an unpublished manuscript by Jean Giraudoux," *Romantic Review*, XLII (1951), 122–34.

———, A Danish Model for Jean Giraudoux, J. P. Jacobsen," *Revue de littérature comparée*, January–March, 1952, pp. 94–105.

———, "Giraudoux's German Studies," *Modern Language Quarterly*, XII (1951), 353–59.

ventional French principles. His enthusiasm and his colorful expression, which reached heights of veritable lyricism, won him many disciples in the literature department. Among them was Jean Giraudoux, who decided to specialize in German studies. Under Andler's guidance Giraudoux read widely and carefully, and when, in 1904, he published his first literary effort, the inspiration of his reading in German is quite apparent.[5] The following year he had the good fortune to secure a traveling fellowship to Germany.

The exhilaration of this young French intellectual, footloose in the magic city of Munich, was still vividly recalled fifteen years or so later in the various versions of *Siegfried*. His adolescent fervor, heightened by poetic reminiscences, caused him to delight in everything he encountered, and he lived happy months with life and literature, dream and reality all run together. His imagination filled the countryside with signs and allusions invisible to others. To others the heather and pines at night might seem common property, but for him

La nuit était ordonnée et tracée comme une nuit d'Albert Dürer. Pas un lapin, pas un lièvre, pas un genièvre et un gibet, avec une grive dans l'angle comme une signature, pas un ruisseau gelé et sillonné d'une rigole à son thalweg, pas une croix, que je ne connusse déjà par le Petit ou le Grand Testament. Nous étions dans ce temps épique du Saint Empire qui continue à vivre en Allemagne le matin, alors que l'époque romantique n'y apparaît que vers midi, et au crépuscule celle du Sturm und Drang. Nous prenions dans l'air le plus frais ce bain de moyen âge que donne la Bavière en sommeil, quand ne circulent encore que les êtres et les animaux qui n'ont pas changé depuis Wallenstein, les belettes, les hermines, les courriers à cheval dont les cors éveillent les chambrières qui entr'ouvrent un volet doucement, et de l'épaule, car il faut empêcher l'autre sein de paraître et le pot de verveine de tomber. Un paysage vu tant de centaines de fois, dans Altdorfer ou dans Wohlgemuth, qu'on s'attendait à apercevoir soudain dans l'air, comme dans leurs dessins et leurs gravures, un gros petit enfant tout nu, ou des mains seules priant, ou des gibets célestes. Une nuit de conjuration, de pillage, qui s'obstinait à ne rien révéler de l'Allemagne moderne.[6]

The Germany which Giraudoux was seeing owed its great charm to Giraudoux's own fancy. Stubbornly blind to modern Germany, he called upon German artists and writers to evoke for him their country. The shades of Hoffmann and company haunted the streets through which Giraudoux sauntered. Paul Morand, whose long and close friendship with Giraudoux dates from their meeting in Munich, testifies that Giraudoux was still steeping himself in Romantic authors. He stresses their important contribution to the future writer's turn of mind: "Les romantiques allemands sont une des sources de son talent. Sans Novalis, sans Jean-Paul Richter surtout, sans Chamisso et La Motte-Fouqué ... la personalité de Giraudoux eût été autre." [7]

On June 23, 1906, the Sorbonne granted Giraudoux the *diplôme d'études supérieures* in German. The following autumn he began working toward the

[5] See item 1 under note 4.

[6] "Siegfried et le Limousin," *Mélanges offerts à Charles Andler* (Publications de la Faculté des Lettres, University of Strasbourg, 1924), XXI, 157–61.

[7] Paul Morand, *Souvenirs* (Geneva: La Palatine, 1948), pp. 132–33.

*agrégation.* It is interesting to note that the program leaned heavily in the direction of the Romantics. For the next few years Giraudoux divided his time between his reading and his career as a young writer. He became a familiar figure at the Café Vachette where Moréas had presided for many years and where writers and students met to discuss their literary theories and convictions. It was not until 1911 when he entered the government service that he renounced definitively his ambition to become an *agrégé.* He had spent seven years in everyday contact with German writers, seven very important years which formed his literary habits and laid the foundation for his entire career.

## The new Romanticism

In the Latin Quarter around 1910 budding authors were advocating further elaboration of Symbolist doctrines and the hasty liquidation of nineteenth-century Realism. They were banded together, not so much through common inspiration as through a spirit of revolt, antipathy toward the stereotyped prose which was their heritage. Many, like Giraudoux, had traveled, and had experienced abroad the revelation of literary ideals foreign to those maintained in France. Upon their return these young writers had found only Symbolism worthy of retention. The reform which Symbolism had begun in poetry should now be applied to prose. The already moribund Realistic tradition had to be destroyed. Giraudoux declared with vehemence "Je n'apprécie à aucun degré la littérature réaliste." [8] We have his own testimony for the literary climate of 1910:

Vers 1910, 1912, il y avait des jeunes gens qui peut-être préparaient, comme moi, l'Ecole normale: ils n'avaient pas la mine de révolutionnaires. Ces jeunes gens se sont mis à voyager. Ils ont échappé à l'influence stérilisante de Paris, où l'homme de lettres était à cette époque une sorte de fonctionnaire exécutant sa besogne dans des cadres tracés une fois pour toutes. Ils ont plongé dans de grandes ondes poétiques dont les cercles de dressage littéraire et mondain semblaient ignorer l'existence. Je ne veux pas dire que la France tout entière se tenait à l'écart du mouvement: il s'était déjà manifesté, en poésie, par Verlaine, Rimbaud et le symbolisme. Mais la prose était figée dans le moule stéréotypé de langage que nous avaient légué le dix-huitième et le dix-neuvième siècles, coupables d'avoir desséché et compliqué le beau langage vivant du dix-septième et du seizième. Et la littérature romanesque était une route monotone, creusée d'ornières dans lesquelles on s'engageait docilement à la queue-leu-leu ... Nous avons voulu réagir, briser les moules, donner du champ à l'invention.[9]

Fresh from his German contacts, the "grandes ondes poétiques," Giraudoux turned a harsh eye upon his own literary heritage. The poetic spirit, "beau colibri étouffé par ces abominables Zola et autres, adeptes du réel," [10] seemed to him the most characteristic quality of the French race. Yet since the eighteenth century, French writers have suppressed all poetic expression. At that time the French language, so rich, mysterious, poetic, was turned into a language of combat. It was

---

[8] Frédéric Lefèvre, *Une Heure avec ...* (Gallimard, 1924), I, 147.
[9] Simonne Ratel, *Dialogues à une seule voix* (Le Tambourin, 1930), p. 12.
[10] "Soliloque sur la colonne de juillet," *Nouvelles littéraires,* August 17, 1929, p. 4.

made clear, limpid, and precise to the prejudice of all other virtues. Even French Romanticism had effected no real emancipation.

The discovery of German Romanticism brought home sharply to the new generation the shortcoming of their own. From the first contact, the young writers, simultaneously discovering Baudelaire and Gérard de Nerval, turned their back on official French Romanticism. The poetry which had nourished them before now lost all savor. *Le Lac, La Tristesse d'Olympio* seemed merely banal and vain. The strophes of Lamartine, Hugo, fell to the level of oratorical generalities and rhymed commonplaces. But Novalis uncovered for their dazzled eyes a new world, a world of limitless perspectives. They felt transported into a mysterious higher zone where ultimate reality and the totality of nature might be perceived. In their enthusiasm, all other poetic efforts seemed gross and senseless in comparison.[11] Giraudoux, who may again be taken for their spokesman, reproaches the Romantic movement of the early nineteenth century for understanding so little of the fundamental principles of Romanticism. Scornfully he dubs it a counterfeit Romanticism:

Celui de 1830 n'était qu'un faux romantisme, une révolution de carton-pâte, un bric-à-brac du moyen âge et du monde entier. Il n'a aucun caractère original, c'est-à-dire national: il n'est fait que d'imitation. Aucun poète n'est moins romantique que Victor Hugo. Vigny est un penseur qui n'atteint à la poésie que par hasard, en passant. Chez Lamartine, peut-être, des traces de vrai romantisme. Mais la plupart des poètes de cette époque sont à la remorque de la poésie artificielle du XVIII^e siècle. Aucune émancipation de fond.[12]

But now at long last French literature is on the brink of Romanticism: "Le romantisme français commence à Verlaine, dans la poésie. Dans le roman, nous en voyons l'aube. Le xx^e siècle sera le siècle romantique par excellence." [13] The French language is finding again its lost qualities:

Le travail ingrat et méritoire a été fait par les symbolistes, puis est venue la génération de Gide, de Claudel et de Proust auxquels les jeunes écrivains se rattachent plutôt par la sympathie et l'admiration que par l'imitation. *Aujourd'hui la littérature française a surtout une valeur morale et poétique, beaucoup plus que de divertissement.*[14]

The emancipated writers of Jena and Heidelberg could offer models and inspiration for a genuine French Romanticism. Novalis, Tieck, and the Schlegel brothers had already enunciated the literary ideal in preaching a free and instinctive existence beyond the walls of the eighteenth-century stronghold of the *Aufklärung*. The course for the new generation was already charted. To revitalize French prose and sweep away the debris of Realism, a reaffirmation of the German Romantic credo was plainly called for. Thus Giraudoux, keenly aware of the similarity between the German revolt and the program to which he and his colleagues were dedicating

---

[11] Gabriel Bounoure, "Moment du romantisme allemand," *Le Romantisme allemand* (Marseilles: Les Cahiers du Sud, 1937), p. 10.

[12] Ratel, *op. cit.*, p. 14.

[13] *Ibid.* M. Edmond Jaloux has pointed out the great contribution of Giraudoux in turning the current of French literature away from Realism and into neo-Romanticism. (*Nouvelles littéraires*, September 6, 1924, p. 3.)

[14] Lefèvre, *op. cit.*, I, 147.

themselves, declared that he wrote *Siegfried et le Limousin,* not so much as a novel, but as a pamphlet to point up the necessity of regaining contact with literary Germany. Like his mythical hero Siegfried, Giraudoux set for himself the task of reintroducing poetry into France.

## GIRAUDOUX AND THE ROMANTIC *Weltanschauung*

### Subjectivism

For both Jean Giraudoux and the German Romantics, poetry suggests first of all an attitude toward the universe, a characteristic *Weltanschauung.* "Poesie und Philosophie sind ein untheilbares Ganzes, ewig verbunden." [15] "Die Trennung von Poet und Denker ist nur scheinbar. . . ." [16] The Jena group were first of all literary theorists and they built their critical edifice on a philosophical basis. Underlying their notion of poetry is a philosophy of pure subjectivity: "... *poétique,* c'est-à-dire 'dirigée de l'intérieur vers l'extérieur,' percevant le monde par une création, une imagination libres. ..." [17]

Inspired by the discoveries of the philosophers Fichte and Schelling, the German poets declared their complete liberty to construct the world according to their imagination and fancy. The sole criterion of values should lie within the individual ego. The exterior world possesses no real autonomy and must depend upon the ego for animation and meaning. Thus every man becomes the creator of his own universe. Since the non-ego is a product of the imagination, the world becomes a vast poem which man is constantly inventing. In the defiant assertions of the German Romantics we perceive a thoroughly modern attitude which will find exaggerated expression in our days: William Lovell cries "Ich *selbst* bin das einzige Gesetz in der ganzen Natur!" [18] and Novalis: "Ich bestimme die Welt!" [19] Giraudoux echoes the intense individualism of his predecessors: "Rien n'est vrai de ce que vous acceptez pour tel, la logique seule est absurde, et puisque je suis homme, je suis dieu dans mon arbitraire souverain." [20] His personages are endowed with absolute power to interpret events as they see fit. It suffices that Alcmène considers herself faithful to have remained so. The fact of her infidelity has no importance. Likewise Judith is pure because she believes herself to be. In Giraudoux's universe there can exist no truth other than that which the individual ego admits.

The affirmation of a completely free, unhistorical ego is the Romantic protest against determinism. The liberty to which both contemporary writers and the Germans claim the right is, nevertheless, heavily charged with responsibility, the obligation of the individual to realize utterly and completely his potentialities. In

[15] Friedrich Schlegel, "Über die Philosophie," *Athenaeum* (Berlin: Heinrich Frölich, 1799), II, 21.

[16] Novalis, *Schriften,* ed. Kluckhohn (Leipzig: Bibliogr. Inst., 1928), III, 137.

[17] Albert Béguin, *L'Ame romantique et le rêve* (Corti, 1946), p. 97.

[18] Tieck, *William Lovell* (*Schriften,* Berlin: G. Reimer, 1828, vol. VI, ser. 1, p. 179).

[19] Novalis, *op. cit.,* III, 217.

[20] "Soliloque sur la colonne de juillet."

his course on transcendental philosophy, Friedrich Schlegel studied carefully the problem of liberty. It has always remained a great factor in the Romantic interpretation of life, whether a source of anguish and exultation, as with Nietzsche, or of anguish as with J. P. Sartre and the Existentialist writers.

In the Romantic system, then, the individual imagination is the sole guide to reality. *Phantasie,* that is, poetic imagination, becomes all important: "Der Verstand, sagt der Verfasser der Reden über die Religion, weiß nur von Universum; die Fantasie herrsche, so habt ihr einen Gott. Ganz recht, die Fantasie ist das Organ des Menschen für die Gottheit." [21] Long misprized as the *folle du logis,* the imagination now assumes full rights over the senses and the intellect, whose data can no longer be accepted as unquestionably valid.

### Anti-rationalism

Strong in their convictions of the authority of the subjective ego, Romantic poets refuse to be bound by the routine interpretation of the world founded exclusively upon the data of the intellect and the senses and formalized into a set of rules. In their eyes the so-called objective world exists only as a convention. It is maintained only as a convenience for social relations. Hence they seem to follow special patterns and rhythms, curiously foreign to our customary notions. In Giraudoux, critics were quick to remark a bold disregard for the accepted hierarchy of values. For example, M. Pierre Humbourg described him as a "dynamomètre qui marque du même poids tous les événements de la vie." [22] Conventional categories do not pertain. What seems trivial is emphasized at the expense of the apparently important; the distinctions between living and inanimate nature, between consciousness and unconsciousness are rubbed away: life becomes as capricious as a dream.

As in a dream even the basic concepts upon which orthodox thought rests are violated. Consider the Romantic treatment of such a fundamental of determinism as the concept of time. Novalis, in *Heinrich von Ofterdingen,* upset all canons of common sense by his prophecies and revelations of the future. In the hermit's mysterious book Heinrich can read of his life to come and see the picture of his future sweetheart. Jean Paul rarely chose to tell a tale in chronological order. Giraudoux, too, has permitted himself a wholly personal and whimsical interpretation of time. In *Ondine,* before the astonished court, the illusionist accelerates time and conjures up scenes of the future. The past itself can be modified. Ondine says: "J'oublie toujours que pour les hommes, ce qui a eu lieu ne peut plus ne pas avoir eu lieu." [23]

The Romantic attitude is more than a lighthearted flaunting of the right of fancy. It represents a grave intent to destroy the prestige of all classifications, established by analysis or demonstration and preserved through tradition. The German movement was first of all, as Giraudoux describes the program of his own generation, a

[21] F. Schlegel, "Ideen," *Athenaeum,* III, 5.
[22] Pierre Humbourg, *Jean Giraudoux* (Marseilles: Les Cahiers du Sud, 1926), p. 60.
[23] *Ondine* (Grasset, 1939), Act II, sc. 14.

protest and a negation. The preface to the *Athenaeum* is remarkably lacking in positive assertions. It is an organ of rupture, of denial. The brothers Schlegel directed all their energies toward breaking with the routine spirit of their times, the *Zunftgeist*. Berlin rationalism, the philosophy of Christian Wolff, Nicolai, etc., had reduced the universe to the level of a mechanism which could easily be grasped by the intellect. But A. W. Schlegel insisted that the intelligence can never capture but a part of truth, while sentiment, embracing everything, alone penetrates the mysteries of nature.[24]

Giraudoux was determined to put an end to the already moribund realistic tradition, because he believed that the cult of intellectualism which it implies inhibits the full use of man's gifts and that a great part of life cannot be reduced to the rational or be observed objectively. "La raison ne suffit pas." [25]

Too long the Goddess of Reason had been worshipped in France. There is no other land, Giraudoux claimed, where imagination and invention are not considered indispensable accessories to life, like gas and electricity![26] With tender irony he mocks his former professor's uncritical devotion to reason:

Mais pour la Raison, maître, j'ai peur de t'avoir moins suivi. Que tu nous la dépeignais belle pourtant ... ! Que la terre devenait douce à fouler, la vie douce à vivre, quand on expliquait ce qui s'y passe, affirmais-tu, par la raison! ... Par raison, dès que l'hiver avait fui, le printemps revenait, et, tant l'étoile polaire était bleue, par raison l'on désirait mourir. Que la Seine était belle aux environs des Andelys, quand par raison elle fait douze boucles ... ! Que les femmes étaient belles quand raisonnables elles nous cédaient, leur chapeau avisé écrasé sous elles et les rideaux tirés sur l'intelligente lune! [27]

These poet-philosophers accuse reason of substituting its artificial categories for living reality. Mechanism and habit have turned dynamic nature into inert forms. In a chapter of *Ofterdingen* Novalis pictures the world under the blight of reason. The personage Der Schreiber incarnates the "petrifying and petrified intellect" struggling to maintain the world in illusion. But he is doomed to fail; ultimate verities slip through his figures and theories. In the course of the allegory, Der Schreiber is defeated by Fabel (poetry), whose babbling reveals profound truths, and Ginnistan (imagination). Giraudoux's character Lemançon recalls Der Schreiber:

L'univers était recouvert pour Lemançon plus que pour tout autre d'une croûte verbale qui lui cachait les gouffres du chaos. ... Devant les opérations les plus simples de l'esprit, comme la déduction ou la restriction devant les aventures les plus cataloguées du coeur, comme l'émotion au printemps devant la première cerise—il ne disposait plus que d'un langage faux.[28]

This crust must be penetrated; the automatic must be broken. Such is the first task of poetry: "Denn das ist der Anfang aller Poesie, den Gang und die Gesetze der

---

[24] *Littérature dramatique* (A. Cherbuliez, 1836), II, 329–30.
[25] Ratel, *op. cit.*, p. 14.
[26] *La Française et La France* (Gallimard, 1951), p. 17.
[27] *Juliette au pays des hommes* (Emile-Paul, 1924), pp. 183–84.
[28] *Ibid.*, p. 133.

vernünftig denkenden Vernunft aufzuheben und uns wieder in die schöne Verwirrung der Fantasie, in das ursprüngliche Chaos der menschlichen Natur zu versetzen. . . ." [29] The poet shall rescue man from the error into which he has fallen, open man's eyes which habit and a limited use of his faculties have sealed. This is the sense of Giraudoux's exultant cry: "J'ai détruit la stupide notion de l'usuel, j'ai sapé les communs rapports des choses entre elles, des hommes entre eux!" [30]

### Structure of the world

Once the spell of routine is broken, the universe appears in its primitive clarity. "J'ai rendu au monde la virginité." [31] Man's eyes are open to the true nature of the universe about him. He can perceive the totality of things, comprehend their intimate construction. From Achim von Arnim to Giraudoux, poets have affirmed the existence of a superior world behind the world of phenomena, a world attainable only through the exercise of the imagination. Like Edmée in *Choix des Elues,* who can step from her apartment into an invisible apartment, Romantic poets have access to a second, a purified world of the spirit. In *Suzanne et le Pacifique* this duality of the world is represented by the twin islands.

Phenomena which surround man in nature assume the character of symbols, finite expressions of infinity. They suggest to him the archetypes, the essences. This realm of the absolute beckons all Romantic poets. Novalis presents the Sais disciples as conceiving of nature as a vast miscellany of signs which man must learn to read before he can penetrate the riddle of existence. In his *Fragmente* he says: "Die Welt ist ein Universaltropus des Geistes, ein symbolisches Bild desselben." [32] Baudelaire will echo this notion in his *Etude sur Delacroix:* "Tout l'univers visible n'est qu'un magasin d'images ou de signes auxquels l'imagination donnera une place et une valeur relative; c'est une espèce de pâture que l'imagination doit digérer et transformer." [33]

Only in so far as phenomena bear witness to the eternal do they capture Giraudoux's interest. Their concrete particularity is for him less real than their capacity for abstraction. Persons are important for what they represent in the world of essences. Thus an evil person is significant only as an incarnation of vice, a hero only an example of heroism, a father only as an example of paternity. The obsession of the absolute accounts for Giraudoux's oft-remarked predilection for the superlative. His work is a great hymn to the maximum, the most perfect, that is to say, the nearest physical approach to the abstract. Whether it be a landscape or a person, all the countless imperfect copies are ignored, cast in the shadow before the brilliance of the unique illustration of the eternal prototype. All Giraudoux's personages are model, verging on abstractions: Simon le pathétique, Jacques le fataliste, etc.

[29] F. Schlegel, "Rede über die Mythologie," *Athenaeum,* III, 103.
[30] "Soliloque sur la colonne de juillet."
[31] *Ibid.*
[32] Novalis, *op. cit.,* II, 384.
[33] Baudelaire, *Oeuvres complètes* (Conard, 1925), III, 12.

They scarcely possess human density, these rarified creatures who so transparently expose the generality from which they spring. This, according to Novalis, is to "romanticize": "Indem ich dem Gemeinen einen hohen Sinn, dem Gewöhnlichen ein geheimnisvolles Ansehn, dem Bekannten die Würde des Unbekannten, dem Endlichen einen unendlichen Schein gebe, so romantisiere ich es." [34]

The archetypes give the universe its basic unity and organization. Manifesting themselves through scattered fragments of phenomena, they impose a system entirely foreign to the rational and logical order which man has erroneously attributed to nature. Mysterious parallels and subtle groupings cut across conventional divisions, identifying themselves with the essences which define the nature of things. The eternal pattern, composed of secret harmonies and affinities in nature, is revealed to the poet through the law of analogy:

Er merkte bald auf die Verbindungen in allem, auf Begegnungen, Zusammentreffungen. Nun sah er bald nichts mehr allein.—In große bunte Bilder drängten sich die Wahrnehmungen seiner Sinne: er hörte, sah, tastete und dachte zugleich. Er freute sich, Fremdlinge zusammen zu bringen. Bald waren ihm die Sterne Menschen, bald die Menschen Sterne, die Steine Tiere, die Wolken Pflanzen. . . .[35]

De grandes ressemblances balafrent le monde et marquent ici et là leur lumière. Elles rapprochent, elles assortissent ce qui est petit et ce qui est immense. D'elles seules peut naître toute nostalgie, tout esprit, toute émotion. Poète? je dois l'être: elles seules me frappent.[36]

Through this law the poet can perceive the eternal in transitory phenomena.

### The place of poetry and the poet

The poet's mission is to exploit his intuitive gifts and lead man to a more complete knowledge of himself and the universe.

Es gab zu allen Zeiten eine Heimlichkeit der Welt, die mehr wert. . . . Wir nennen diese Einsicht, wenn sie sich mitteilen läßt, Dichtung. . . .[37]

Poetry, long considered as an agreeable, but trivial pastime, becomes an instrument of metaphysical inquiry. Klingsohr, in *Ofterdingen,* claims that it is the most natural and the most complete of the activities of the mind, the deepest knowledge and the highest art.[38] Giraudoux declares: "C'est à la poésie, à elle seule que seront toujours réservées la navigation et la découverte." [39]

The poet becomes a seer. He alone has the power to render the superior world visible; he is the nexus between the two zones of the universe. As Giraudoux implies above, this lofty conception of art and the belief that the artist is a sort of prophet empowered to reveal mysteries enters modern French literature with

---

[34] Novalis, *op. cit.,* II, 335.

[35] *Ibid.,* I, 12.

[36] Giraudoux, *L'Ecole des indifférents* (Grasset, 1910), p. 73.

[37] Arnim, Introduction to *Die Kronenwächter* (*Werke,* Leipzig, critical edition of Alfred Schier, n. d., I, 15–16).

[38] Chapter VII.

[39] "Choderlos de Laclos," *Littérature* (Grasset, 1941), p. 65.

Rimbaud (Il faut être voyant). But it was of course already systematically developed by the Germans much earlier. Schelling taught that art represents the highest stage of human evolution and Arnim said, "Nennen wir die heiligen Dichter auch Seher." [40] Novalis proclaimed over and over again that the poet understands nature better than the scientist, that only an artist can understand the meaning of existence. He is the veritable initiated one, the mage who remains in intimate communion with nature. Poet and priest are synonymous: "Dichter und Priester waren im Anfang eins. . . . Der echte Dichter ist aber immer Priester." [41]

Giraudoux places himself in the category of the mages by announcing: "Je suis le sourcier de l'Eden, etc. ..." [42] He can conceive of artistic creation only as the work of a demiurge. All great authors are diviners. They do not tarry to describe or analyze, but strike directly at the *Ding an sich*. Through flashes of insight, they grasp and record the total and intimate nature of the object of their investigation. Consider La Fontaine before his animals:

Ce n'est pas qu'il les ait étudiés et copiés, c'est qu'un animal créé de toutes pièces par La Fontaine contient une part de vérité suffisante qui est la vérité de La Fontaine. La Fontaine a compris les animaux parce qu'il avait le sentiment du vol, de la fuite, de la chaleur animales, et de même il a compris les plantes et les eaux parce qu'il avait le senti-ment de l'ondulation, du frémissement et de la plainte.[48]

## GIRAUDOUX AND THE ROMANTIC *Kunstanschauung*

### The poet and his work

The Romantic esthetic is built upon the Romantic conception of the universe and the role of the poet as transcendental revealer.[44] The act of artistic creation takes place during those times when he feels in a state of intimate contact with the forces of nature. At certain moments he is possessed by wonderful illuminations which permit him to penetrate beyond the exteriority of things. These instants of privilege have been described by the German poets who experienced them. They feel over-come by a remarkable transfiguration in which the physical and spiritual aspects of their being seem to melt into one—they behold their fundamental unity. Jean Paul's works testify to the constant joyous wonder he experienced before nature, the all-pervading optimism and beatitude. He writes as if in a wonderful dream. We may imagine him at his writing table before the open window on a May morning: "Alles grüne—alles dufte—ich schaue nach einem unter der Sonne blitzenden Turmknopf hinaus, ruhend im Fenster eines weißen Gartenhäuschens, die Augen-lider voll Blumenstaub, die Achseln voll dünne Kirschenblüten, die Ohren voll

---

[40] Arnim, *op. cit.*, p. 16.
[41] Novalis, *op. cit.*, II, 26.
[42] *Juliette au pays des hommes*, pp. 191–92.
[43] *Les Cinq Tentations de La Fontaine* (Grasset, 1938), pp. 50–52.
[44] Giraudoux's antipathy toward Realism precludes any notion of art as imitation as far as he is concerned. As for the Germans, they had revolted against the Aristotelian yoke by proclaiming that art is only creation. See Richter, *Vorschule der Aesthetik;* Schelling, *System des Tranzenden-talen Idealismus;* Schlegel, *Vorlesungen über schöne Literatur und Kunst.*

Gesumse des benachbarten Bienenstandes, . . ."[45] With Novalis, the state of inspiration becomes clearly the ecstasy of the mystics. All extraneous impressions disappear before the revelation. What does it resemble?

Es ist kein Schauen, Hören, Fühlen; es ist aus allen dreien zusammengesetzt, mehr als alles Dreies: eine Empfindung unmittelbarer Gewißheit, eine Ansicht meines wahrhaftesten, eigensten Lebens. Die Gedanken verwandeln sich in Gesetze, die Wünsche in Erfüllungen.

What serves as stimulus for such phenomena?

Auffallend wird die Erscheinung besonders beim Anblick mancher menschlichen Gestalten und Gesichter, vorzüglich bei der Erblickung mancher Augen, mancher Mienen, mancher Bewegungen, beim Hören gewisser Worte, beim Lesen gewisser Stellen, bei gewissen Hinsichten auf Leben, Welt und Schicksal. . . .

Certain seasons and hours have the power to induce the spell. It is usually of very brief duration.[46]

The poetic experience as recorded by Novalis is not unlike Proust's celebrated visions of the Martinville steeples, etc. Baudelaire, too, was privileged to know the same mysterious state of grace. He describes it at the beginning of the *Poème du Haschisch* under the title "Le Goût de l'Infini." It is interesting that he should preface his account with an allusion to other records of such moments, citing particularly Hoffmann. The rhapsodical terms of his description follow the German pattern:

Il est des jours où l'homme s'éveille avec un génie jeune et vigoureux. Ses paupières à peine déchargées du sommeil qui les scellait, le monde extérieur s'offre à lui avec un relief puissant, une netteté de contours, une richesse de couleurs admirables. Le monde moral ouvre ses vastes perspectives, pleines de clartés nouvelles. L'homme gratifié de cette béatitude, malheureusement rare et passagère, se sent à la fois plus artiste et plus juste, plus noble. ... Mais ce qu'il y a de plus singulier dans cet état exceptionel de l'esprit et des sens, que je puis sans exagération appeler paradisiaque, si je le compare aux lourdes ténèbres de l'existence commune et journalière, c'est qu'il n'a été créé par aucune cause bien visible et facile à définir. Nous sommes obligés de reconnaître que souvent cette merveille, cette espèce de prodige, se produit comme si elle était l'effet d'une puissance supérieure et invisible, extérieure à l'homme. ... C'est pourquoi je préfère considérer cette condition anormale de l'esprit comme une véritable grâce ... une espèce d'excitation angélique ... le souvenir des réalites invisibles.[47]

Jean Giraudoux offers abundant testimony to his experiences. They appear to him moments out of time and space in which he feels in complete harmony with the universe and capable of understanding life's meaning. They are accompanied by a strong sense of being, infinite liberty, acute sensibility and lucidity. In a state of euphoria, the subject slips out of the human condition to dominate his destiny.[48]

[45] J. P. Richter, *Des Quintus Fixlein Leben* (*Deutsche National-Literatur*, Berlin, Spemann, n. d., CXXXI, 151).

[46] *Op. cit.*, II, 18.

[47] *Oeuvres complètes*, X, 3–5.

[48] Mr. Gunnar Høst cites numerous instances in Giraudoux's work where the poetic moment is described. See Høst, *L'Oeuvre de Jean Giraudoux* (Oslo: H. Aschehoug, 1942), Chapter XIII.

In *Intermezzo,* before the phenomenon of a town apparently bewitched, the supervisor exclaims, "Notre ville est folle." The druggist replies, "Elle est bien plutôt dans cet état où tous les voeux s'exaucent, où toutes les divagations se trouvent être justes. Chez un individu, cela s'appelle l'état poétique." [49]

Recording what he experiences at such times does not constitute for the poet any conscious effort. He feels himself merely a passive agent obeying a power superior to his own will. Jean Paul Richter is the first of the Romantics to articulate clearly a definition of inspiration. He observed that the true poet, as he creates, is only the listener, not the master. Novalis claimed that "der Dichter ordnet, vereinigt, wählt, erfindet—und es ist ihm selbst unbegreiflich, warum gerade so und nicht anders." [50] With bitter anguish Achim von Arnim ruminated the problem of whether what he wrote really belonged to him; he came to the conclusion that art is a game which the artist practices without comprehending its implications. Therefore the writer should accept without reservation all which is dictated to him. For this relinquishment of intellectual control over what he wrote the surrealists hail Arnim as a precursor. By the same token he is also a precursor of Giraudoux.

Writing, according to Giraudoux's own statement of his method, is not in any sense labor, but rather a natural function of the poet: "... et rien ne devrait plus ressembler à ce qu'écrit un spirite que ce qu'écrit un écrivain." He claims no responsibility for what he writes. For months he will not touch pen to paper: "J'ai l'impression d'attendre une espèce de commande. Elle vient je ne sais pourquoi." [51] Giraudoux's divulgences sound very similar to those of Schiller, the spiritual father of the Romantic generation. A sort of vague musical atmosphere prompts their creation. Schiller said that when he began to write, it was usually the musical element and not a clear concept of the subject which came first.[52] Giraudoux believed writers should compose like musicians "... L'ambiance, l'atmosphère se créent et c'est là-dessus que je travaille. Ce que j'écris correspond à un thème général, mais avant d'avoir tracé le premier mot j'ignore ce que ce sera." [53]

Since the creative fury cannot be commanded, the poet must patiently await its visitation. Idleness is imposed upon him as a requisite of his art. Industry has no value, no meaning to the creative personality. In *Lucinde* Friedrich Schlegel makes the apology of nonchalance in regard to his work. He endorses a contemplative idleness in opposition to exterior effort and activity which would hinder genius from operating spontaneously. Perhaps one should interpret Schlegel's exposition as a sort of rationalization, knowing how hard it was for him to work methodically. Earning his living by the pen had its irksome aspects. But it does illustrate the important place he assigns to intuition and the disdain he felt toward form and craftsmanship.

[49] Act II, sc. 1.
[50] *Op. cit.,* III, 349.
[51] C. Charensol, "Comment écrivez-vous, Jean Giraudoux?" *Nouvelles littéraires,* December 19, 1931, p. 8.
[52] *Schillers Briefe* (Stuttgart: Deutsche Verlags-Anstalt, n. d.), III, 202.
[53] Charensol, *op. cit.*

Georg Brandes [54] traces the Romantic endorsement of idleness back to Herder's objection to the notion of purpose or aim in history. Herder believed that what happens has a cause and is subject to laws, but cannot be explained by anything which has not yet happened, i.e., by a purpose. Transferred into the personal and esthetic domain, this means a work of art is purposeless and its author a spontaneous and "idle" genius. The apology for idleness found favor with such writers as Kierkegaard, who systematized it in *Enter-Eller* (Never adopt a profession, etc.), and Eichendorff, who idealized it in *Taugenichts*. Brandes calls such a view a caricature of a philosophy, but the Romantics found it useful in combatting eighteenth-century utilitarianism. Schlegel would even exalt idleness to the status of a cosmic force! "In der Tat, man sollte das Studium des Müßiggangs nicht so sträflich vernachlässigen, sondern es zur Kunst und Wissenschaft, ja zur Religion bilden!" [55]

The faith in inspiration makes spontaneity a first principle in the Romantic esthetic. Convinced of the supreme validity of their intuitive genius, poets from Jean Paul to Jean Giraudoux eschew all effort which might suppress or modify their free expression. Giraudoux believed that it is the element of improvisation which gives life to a work, and which gives it poetry. This is the secret of his art: "On a dit que j'écrivais sans une rature. C'est vrai. Je n'ai qu'à me laisser aller, et pourquoi me reprendrais-je? Mes manuscrits sont nets comme un lis, comme une vitre, comme une vierge. Et ce mot contient, si l'on veut savoir, tout le secret de mon art." [56] All correction and alteration must be rigorously guarded against to preserve the freshness and integrity of the poetic vision.

The imperfections and extravagances which are inevitable in a procedure free from the care of composition or any studied control are not only regarded indulgently, but valued as evidence of naturalness and sincerity. In the name of these virtues, Giraudoux, in characteristic paradox, takes his own national literature to task:

La littérature française en effet n'est pas une expression. Elle ne comporte aucun naturel, et le style français le plus naturel, mettons celui de Voltaire, est justement celui qui pousse notre esprit et notre langue à leur pire artifice, en leur refusant des excès, préciosité ou gongorisme, qui correspondent du moins à de vrais défauts ou qualités humaines. [57]

Giraudoux could find in Jean Paul a worthy model for his native exuberance. The latter confessed engagingly that he was powerless to control his pen, that his "figures and illustrations were like mice let out of a trap, one caught hold of the tail of the other in interminable succession." [58] The similarity between these two expansive talents has been frequently remarked. M. Maurice Bourdet pointed out that Richter already possessed Giraudoux's characteristic phrasings:

[54] *Main Currents in Nineteenth Century Literature* (New York: Macmillan, n. d.), II, 21. (See also Chapter VI.)

[55] "Idylle über den Müßiggang," *Lucinde* (Aubier, 1943), p. 92.

[56] "Soliloque sur la colonne de juillet."

[57] "Charles-Louis Philippe," *Littérature*, p. 90.

[58] Cited by E. B. Lee, *Life of J. P. F. Richter* (Boston: Ticknor and Fields, 1864), p. 491. (Source not given.)

Quant à Jean-Paul, on ne peut parfois maîtriser son étonnement, en relisant *Quintus Fix-lein,* par exemple, de retrouver en lui certaines tournures de phrases à la Giraudoux, comme celle-ci «La lune qui a été en quelque sorte le cachet opposé à son bonheur d'hier et qui a perdu son éclat lumineux, plonge dans l'Occident comme un seau vide tandis qu'à l'Orient s'élève le deuxième seau rempli jusqu'au bord. ...» Dépouillons la phrase de cette teinte d'un romantisme à la Rousseau et voici une impression pour *Provinciales.*[59]

Hence the Romantic interest in first sketches, the *Rohstoff.* Tieck declared that he preferred the works of great poets written before their style was developed or which they chose to leave formless. Giraudoux finds the notes for even mediocre novels interesting. In the rough draft the poet retains the fluidity, the mobility which he ascribes to nature. It appears a living and growing thing in contrast to the dead perfection of a masterpiece. Giraudoux invented a phrase: "ennuyeux comme un chef-d'oeuvre."[60] "Les chefs-d'oeuvre sont les statues de la littérature et en encombrent les voies."[61] He reminded Lefèvre: "Mais vous savez bien que je n'aime guère les chefs-d'oeuvre."[62] Friedrich Schlegel had said "An der Form liegt nichts."[63] The Romanticists jealously guard their expression from assuming a finite form in order to remain in the live currents of the infinite. This is the essential difference, according to Schlegel, between Romantic *Dichtung* and all other. Other artistic productions are finished and can be encompassed. But the Romantic work is always in the process of becoming. It can never be completed. It is ever-lasting; it is completely free.[64]

The theory of the masterpiece, as illustrated in French literature by a Flaubert, is, moreover, wholly incompatible with the Romantic notion of the nature of a work of art. Art is never an end in itself, we must remember, but an instrument of discovery and knowledge. Thus it is a matter of little concern if Novalis, Schlegel, and the others left their work fragmentary and unfinished. Giraudoux could not conceive of a work as a unit, finished once and for all. Around his major undertakings such as *Siegfried,* he multiplied *plaquettes* and different versions. The Romanticists regarded their works primarily as means of self-expression, self-seeking, creation. Novalis said: "Ich behandle meine Schriftstellerei nur als Bildungsmittel."[65] Giraudoux found little interest in a work of art independent of the artist who created it. He confessed to Frédéric Lefèvre that his greatest enjoyment of literature was the revelation it affords of the artistic personality behind the work. With Rimbaud in

[59] Bourdet, *Jean Giraudoux* (La Nouvelle Revue critique, 1928), pp. 51–52. Jean Cassou has made a collection of Jean Paul's rhetorical gems which remind him of Giraudoux. *Pour la Poésie* (Corrêa, 1935), p. 108.
[60] André Beucler, "Vie et Mort de Jean Giraudoux," *Confluences* (Hommage à Jean Giraudoux), 1945, p. 107.
[61] *Littérature,* p. 190.
[62] Lefèvre, *op. cit.,* IV, 117. (Note Souday's references to this remark as being nothing but paradox and mystification! *Le Temps,* August 19, 1926.)
[63] *Athenaeum,* vol. I, ser. 2, p. 72.
[64] *Ibid.,* pp. 29–30.
[65] *Op. cit.,* IV, 329.

mind especially, he concluded that "l'écriture est un accident dans la vie du poète." [66]
The word poet does not describe a profession, a skill, or an art, but the highest and
purest life to which man can aspire. Benefits of this life—the poetic experience, the
fleeting intuitions into the nature of things—these are what the Romanticist seeks
to achieve in his own work and what he looks for in another's.

### The poetic genre

With their insistence upon spontaneity and their admiration for unpolished art, it
is not surprising that the Romanticists would be little given to verse as a medium
of expression. A fragment from Goethe summarizes the Romantic point of view.
Form and formality are so inimical to Jean Paul's conception of his art, Goethe says,
that the poet confessed he could never compose a single verse.[67] To Giraudoux, the
exigencies of French prosody appeared shackles to the spontaneous expression of
lyricism and whimsy which he deemed the fundamental necessity of poetry. "Poète?
Dieu me préserve de faire des vers, d'écrire ce que je pense en lignes, de passer à
leur laminoir ma vie." [68] Like the Germans before him, Giraudoux turned to the
prose genres to find the freedom which he demanded. They could show him how to
renovate the novel and its minor forms by turning them from realism into paths of
poesy and phantasy.

In Giraudoux's hands the French novel departs abruptly from the prose tradition
developed in the nineteenth century. He depicts no precise society, he tells no story;
his characters resemble no one and no discernible structure or plan exists to sustain
his writing. In short, he rejects all properties of conventional fiction and dedicates
himself to creating the poetic novel of the twentieth century. Madame Claude-
Edmonde Magny will grant Giraudoux only the modest title of "herald of the
poetic novel." I do not understand her reservations. To be sure, Giraudoux opened
the novel to poetry, but it is difficult to see how anyone could more fully realize the
genre of the poetic novel *per se*. It would seem rather that already today the trend
is reverting toward greater realism. Giraudoux's rôle was to free the novel from its
nineteenth-century strait jacket; but, all due allowance being made for the gratitude
of younger writers, no one has challenged his position.

Giraudoux's novel stands more as a fulfillment than as a prophecy. Its theory and
technique were already elaborately developed by the German Romanticists. Madame
Magny fails to take them into account when she states: "Aussi, le roman précieux à
la Giraudoux ouvre-t-il la voie à un genre auquel nul écrivain ne s'est encore
appliqué de façon systématique: le roman poétique." [69] The poetic novel was the
main obsession of these writers, and their common goal.

---

[66] Lefèvre, *op. cit.*, IV, 122. (Cf. Lamartine's statement: "La poésie n'était pas mon métier;
c'était un accident, une aventure heureuse, une bonne fortune dans ma vie." Preface to the
*Recueillements.*)

[67] *Goethes Gespräche*, ed. F. W. V. Biedermann (Leipzig, 1909), I, 290.

[68] *L'Ecole des indifférents*, pp. 71–72.

[69] Claude-Edmonde Magny, *Précieux Giraudoux* (Editions du Seuil, 1945), p. 76.

Examination of some of the chief works of the period reveals that their approach is substantially the same as Giraudoux's. Professor Baldensperger, in commenting upon the "structure" of Giraudoux's narrative, is reminded of the German school:

Il va de soi qu'en principe la forme narrative, propre à une telle esthétique, ne pouvait être le roman façonné par les sociétés occidentales: c'est bien de «contes» qu'est fait l'oeuvre la plus significative de Giraudoux, au sens que le «märchen» prenait sous la plume des nonchalants narrateurs, pour qui l'essentiel était de permettre à une «dissonance» de s'atténuer ou de s'aggraver: et dans le drame subtil résidait, plus que dans tout résultat matériel, l'intérêt de ces «bouts-rimés» comme Novalis appelle le roman tel qu'il l'admet dans son esthétique.[70]

The "nonchalant narrators" knew nothing of composition in the conventional sense. In *Godwi,* Brentano shows complete inability or indifference in the matter of creating a plot or following through an idea. The action in Jean Paul's novels stumbles and loses its way in a tangle of asides and digressions. *Quintus Fixlein* is without a central subject. Friedrich Schlegel, in his *Brief über den Roman,* defends Jean Paul whose work was accused of not being a novel because it lacks a straightforward plot and reveals too patently the personality of the author. He insisted that the novel is first of all a personal expression: ". . . daß das Beste in den besten Romanen nichts anderes ist als ein mehr oder minder verhülltes Selbstbekenntnis der Verfassers, der Ertrag seiner Erfahrung, die Quintessenz seiner Eigentümlichkeit." [71] The Romantic objective in the novel, as Schlegel saw it, is "was uns einen sentimentalen Stoff in einer phantastischen Form darstellt." [72] He demanded that the form of the novel be an arabesque, that is, whimsical and musical. As it progresses it spreads into countless digressions. The personality of the author is the only center for this growing and expanding organism. Each chapter prepares for the following one. Schlegel compared this type of development to that of a musical composition with its weaving themes and motifs.[73] In his own work *Lucinde* he hoped to establish a model for the Romantic novel. Utterly devoid of chronological or logical order, continuity of action, it appears as a negligent collection of effusions and reflections. From the point of view of structure, it is pure anarchy, truly "an extravagant little book" as he himself described it.[74]

Narration was with the Germans an aspect of purely secondary importance. The novel is first of all, as Edmond Jaloux states, "un véhicule philosophique, un véhicule moral, un véhicule lyrique; ils ne racontent pas pour raconter, mais pour entreprendre une aventure considérable dans le domaine de l'esprit." [75] Hence the novelist is permitted all liberty to organize his material as he chooses. He has only to abandon himself to the evocations of his creative imagination. If the reason is shocked in its conventional notions, so much the worse. What the Romantics wish

[70] Baldensperger, *op. cit.,* p. 6.
[71] *Athenaeum,* III, 126.
[72] *Ibid.,* p. 119.
[73] See p. 17.
[74] Introduction to *Lucinde,* p. 9.
[75] Edmond Jaloux, *Du Rêve à la réalité* (Corrêa, 1932), p. 131.

to represent in their art is life in its integrity without mutilation imposed by reason. The unity of their work is that of life itself with its constant flux of creation and renewal, its marvelous irrationality. The novel, Novalis wrote, treats of life, is a representation of life. . . . As such, it contains no predetermined result, it is not the image of a proposition. The only unity it needs have is one of spirit or tone. M. Jaloux is reminded of many contemporary French prose works. Their unity depends entirely, he says, upon "une certaine couleur que l'on donne à un récit." [76]

Giraudoux put himself unequivocally in the German camp to oppose the Flaubert tradition. "Notre prose a été abîmée par le soin de la composition." He mocked the patient novelists who, "binocle au nez, s'occupent à assembler en un roman, comme un jeu de patience, mille pensées qu'ils n'ont eues que séparément." [77] *Siegfried et le Limousin* was written in twenty-seven days:

Je prends une feuille blanche et je commence à écrire; les personnages naissent au fur et à mesure; au bout de cinq ou six pages, j'y vois clair. ... D'ailleurs, je ne considère tout ce que j'ai fait que comme une espèce de divagation poétique, et je n'ai jamais eu la prétention de faire un roman ou une composition littéraire quelconque. [78]

Although Giraudoux is spoken of as a novelist and author of *nouvelles,* he is in no sense a narrator. The slender narrative is everywhere subservient to description, or rather to evocation of scenes and *états d'âme.* Episodes are quickly dealt with by means of a few imprecise but suggestive strokes. Always his manner is subjective and impressionistic, one of poetic vagaries. His text is in complete agreement with the German specifications for the content of a novel. Its material should be the revelation of an individual conscience, the record of a spiritual life. In the Romantic novel external events can claim a place only incidental to psychological situations.

The nonchalance in the matter of plot is equally evident in the presentation of characters. Tieck was apparently unable to create characters. They are cerebral products, without flesh and blood. The many characters which appear in his books are as shadowy as magic lantern figures. [79]

Friedrich Schlegel explained the Romantic failure to represent characters in lifelike dimensions on the grounds that the Romantic objective lies beyond the pure and simple representation of man, his passions and his acts. Well-described and interesting characters, he says, are not enough to make a book great. The Romantic novel, conceived of as an intimate confession and wholly concerned with the inner world of the author, does not lend itself to the objective or exhaustive depiction of characters. [80] Novalis said of his Ofterdingen: "*Passive* Natur des Romanhelden. Er ist das Organ des Dichters im Roman." [81] Giraudoux states his position: "J'écris toujours à la première personne parce que je ne veux pas faire l'artifice de créer un

---

[76] *Ibid.,* p. 121.
[77] *L'Ecole des indifférents,* pp. 119–20.
[78] Lefèvre, *op. cit.,* I, 149.
[79] Ricarda Huch, *Die Romantik* (Leipzig: H. Hässel, 1913), I, 117.
[80] See note 71.
[81] *Op. cit.,* III, 324.

autre personnage." [82] Those which cannot be identified directly with their creator's personality represent his obsessions, and, devoid of particularity, blend into a character type. The angelic *Mädchen* of Jean Paul and the *jeunes filles* of Giraudoux are but many copies of the model of young womanhood.

As Professor Baldensperger has observed, the genre most suitable to the Romantic purpose lay in the direction of the *Märchen*. Goethe's experiments had led the way back to the old German fairy tale, and Friedrich Schlegel urged Romantic authors to seek inspiration from such fresh sources. The *Märchen* could show them the spontaneity and the blending of conscious and unconscious elements which they required of a work of art. Devoid of logical articulation, its only causality seems akin to that of the dream. It develops like a musical improvisation as it recounts its marvelous things and happenings. Novalis, recognizing in the *Märchen* the vehicle par excellence where poetic inspiration could find adequate expression, asserted: "Das Märchen ist gleichsam der *Kanon der Poesie*—alles Poetische muß märchenhaft sein." [83] The major German authors cultivated the genre with enthusiasm. The best of their work comes to us in this form, so ideally adapted to present their blendings of reality and fancy, narration and lyricism.

Giraudoux's admiration for the *Märchen* is evident especially in his early works. The student essay which appeared in the *Marseille-Etudiant* is a fantastic tale à la Hoffmann. *Les Provinciales* and *L'Ecole des Indifférents* contain examples reminiscent in form and subject of the *Märchen* as adapted by the nineteenth-century Romantics. His pen seems to follow its own way through meandering recollection and daydreaming as it evokes poetic scenes of village life and schoolboy days. It fulfills Novalis' description: "Erzählungen, ohne Zusammenhang, jedoch mit Assoziation, wie *Träume*." [84] Like the Germans, Giraudoux exploited the lore of his province. *Sainte Estelle,* for example, is the story of a local saint. The books of Henri Pourrat (*Gaspard* and *A la belle Bergère*) delighted Giraudoux for their quaint and fantastic qualities. He often thought of trying to revive all those legendary characters.

*The* Märchen *as an exemplification of the Romantic ideal*

It is in relation to the *Märchen* that the Romantic school declared most vehemently its literary aspirations and reveals its peculiar character. The qualities which the German poets discovered in the *Märchen* established the fundamentals of all Romantic *Dichtung*. It is their highest standard of measuring literary values, their illustrious precursor, and their model.

The *Märchen* appealed to the Romantics primarily because of its feeling of the marvelous, its fresh and childlike attitude. Its primitiveness gratified their urge to cut back through the crust of civilization and routine to regain intimate contact with nature. Novalis and the others hailed it as a product of a Golden Age, the age

[82] Lefèvre, *op. cit.,* I, 149.
[83] *Op. cit.,* III, 248.
[84] *Ibid.,* p. 323.

of man's innocence, which constantly haunts the Romantic mind. This nostalgia can be traced to Herder, who claimed greatness for all primitive poetry on the basis that it is a true expression of feeling and of the whole soul.[85] His exhortations turned the German writers to a study of their national past in the hope of capturing again the naïveté which inspired the poetry of their ancestors. Klopstock and Goethe made eulogies of folk songs and Gothic architecture. Ludwig Tieck, introduced to the Middle Ages through Wackenroder, was the first to put in actual practice Herder's recommendation and create a new genre by renewing archaic folk tales through the free play of fancy. *Mutatis mutandis,* Giraudoux restates Herder's appeal when he announces that the period of the *chanson de geste* is the greatest period in French literature, and that the novel, the modern heir to the *chanson de geste,* should return to the poetry and fantasy which made the epics great.

According to Romantic notion, primitive man had not yet invented general classifications of objects perceptible to him through his senses or acquired the attitude that they were exterior and independent of his senses. His mind has not yet developed the separate and distinct faculties which Romantics view as a morbid evolution.[86] The more man's faculties are unified, they reasoned, the more the phenomena which he observes are unified, complete, and personal. Man has since lost this perfect integration. Novalis looked fondly back to the time when all his thoughts must have been perfectly fresh and original, all his affirmations a true reflection of nature. He fancied himself as a modern prophet of a *patrie perdue.*

Giraudoux joined the earlier Romantics in nostalgic evocations of primitive happiness, earthly paradise, Garden of Eden, original innocence. In his essay on Charles-Louis Philippe, he dwells on the importance of "innocence in literature." He likes to imagine spots on the globe which are untouched Edens (*Suzanne et le Pacifique*) and takes delight in portraying "innocent" characters. In the celebrated Prière sur la Tour Eiffel he declared his Messianic rôle:

C'est que je vis encore ... dans cet intervalle qui sépara la création et le péché originel. J'ai été excepté de la malédiction en bloc. ... Je suis un petit Messie pour les tâches de soleil. ... Dès que je donnais des signes d'intelligence ou que je bavardais, nous nous approchions du bonheur et du sol primitifs. Il y eut un soir ... où personne ne peut parler que moi, c'est que nous étions campés sur l'affleurement d'un terrain non condamné par Jehovah, c'est que tous étaient heureux. ... Je suis le sourcier de l'Eden![87]

*Literary patterns adopted from the* Märchen

The *Märchen* records the Edenic vision, man's direct and instinctive reaction to the universe. Not having clearly defined the ego and the non-ego, primitive man attributed to all nature a life and personality like his own. As he attempted to depict the eternal forces revealing themselves through nature, he reduced them to his own

[85] L. S. Willoughby, *The Romantic Movement in Germany* (Oxford University Press, 1930), p. 2.

[86] For a discussion of Hoffmann's nostalgia, see Pierre Missac, "Hoffmann et le péché originel," *Le Romantisme allemand,* pp. 308–14.

[87] *Juliette au pays des hommes,* pp. 188–92.

dimensions. He could not conceive of the universe except in his own terms. He had to personalize in order to understand. Therefore the characteristic patterns which Romanticists could observe in the *Märchen* are allegory, symbolism, personification. They adopt them *en bloc* to recapture the naïve point of view.

A large place is reserved for allegory in Romantic esthetics. As early as *Wilhelm Meister* and the nature myths of Goethe, German poets sought to realize its possibilities. Friedrich Schlegel, who pointed out its use in the novel, made a place for it in his *Lucinde*. To him it was the attribute of all beauty, the sole means of expressing the inexpressable. He believed that since all Romantic poetry strives either to substitute something concrete for an abstraction or to tie a concrete form to the idea behind it, symbolism and allegory must be its fundamental processes.

Wie kann nun das Unendliche auf die Oberfläche, zur Erscheinung gebracht werden? Nur symbolisch, in Bildern und Zeichen. Die unpoetische Ansicht der Dinge ist die, welche mit den Wahrnehmungen der Sinne und den Bestimmungen des Verstandes alles an ihnen für abgetan hält; die poetische, welche sie immerfort deutet und eine figürliche Unerschöpflichkeit in ihnen sieht . . . Dadurch wird erst alles für uns lebendig. Dichten (in weitesten Sinne für das Poetische allen Künsten zum Grunde Liegende genommen) ist nichts andres als ein ewiges Symbolisieren: wir suchen entweder für etwas Geistiges eine äussere Hülle, oder wir beziehen ein Äussres auf ein unsichtbares Innres.[88]

Tieck and Novalis made interesting experiments. In Tieck's *Sternbald* the idea recurs again and again that all true art must be allegorical. Inspired by the *autos* of Calderón, Tieck adapted allegory to the theater. In *Kaiser Octavianus* (Prologue) Faith, Love, Bravery, Romance, Humor are all personified. Novalis would make allegory the sole vehicle for conveying meaning in poetry: "Höchstens kann wahre Poesie einen *allegorischen* Sinn . . . haben." [89] It is interesting to see their predilection for allegory sustained by Baudelaire, through whom many German notions moved into France. "L'allégorie, ce genre si *spirituel* ... qui est vraiment l'une des formes primitives et les plus naturelles de la poésie. ..." [90]

Giraudoux confides that from childhood he felt a natural penchant toward the allegory and could not represent abstractions otherwise:

Au nom seul du Jour, je le sentais onduler silencieusement entre ses deux nuits comme un cygne aux ailes noires. Au nom seul du Mois, je le voyais s'échafauder, arc-bouté sur ses Jeudis et ses Dimanches. Je voyais les Saisons, les Vertus marcher en groupes, dormir par dortoirs. J'avais pour le monde entier la tendresse et l'indulgence qu'inspirent les allégories.[91]

The choicest pages of *Provinciales* bear the title *Allégories*. Spring, Nostalgia, Love, Friendship (favorite Romantic themes) are evoked as creatures of flesh and blood. Often, with Giraudoux, the essences themselves boldly appear without disguisement.

---

[88] A. W. Schlegel, "Vorlesungen über schöne Literatur und Kunst," *Deutsche Literatur* (Leipzig: Philipp Reclam, 1931), ser. 17, vol. III, p. 288.
[89] *Op. cit.*, III, 323.
[90] *Oeuvres complètes*, X, 51.
[91] *L'Ecole des indifférents*, p. 42.

War, Pride, etc. are apostrophized and presented as if they were persons. One is everywhere struck by the facility of Giraudoux to slip back and forth between the abstract and the physical. Before your eyes, persons are suddenly metamorphosed into the qualities they represent. Thus a procession of pilgrims becomes a procession of abstractions: "En tête marchait Orgueil, fier de sa faute. ... Puis vint Vanité. ..." [92]

The Romantic penchant toward allegory explains the great interest in mythology. Friedrich Schlegel called attention in the *Athenaeum* to the importance of mythology to poetry: "Denn Mythologie und Poesie, beyde sind Eins und unzertrennlich." [93] To create a Romantic *Dichtung,* he called upon his generation to remember the poetry of the ancients and its relationship to mythology. Schelling, in his *Philosophie der Kunst,* said that every truly creative individual must invent his mythology. Giraudoux's exploitation of classic and religious myths is obvious from his titles alone. He could find no better way to incarnate his abstractions.

### Attitude toward man and nature

The innocent confusion of the inanimate and the animate which marks the *Märchen* is implicit in the hylozoism of primitive man. Everything in the universe is alive; everything has body and soul. All children know that plants and springs and trees are living beings. Schelling, the Romantic philosopher, defended their convictions. Formulating the idea of a single active principle in nature, uniting all phenomena whether organic or inorganic, he concluded that nature and spirit are identical. Romantic writers, always eager to welcome any affirmation of unity in diversity, heartily concurred. Schelling's notion of the *Weltseele* reappears in Giraudoux:

L'âme du monde aspire et expire par les naseaux et les branchies. Mais l'homme a voulu son âme à soi. Il a morcelé stupidement l'âme générale. Il n'y a pas d'âme des hommes. Il n'y a qu'une série de petits lots d'âme où poussent de maigres fleurs et de maigres légumes. [94]

Novalis and Tieck especially illustrated Schelling's pantheistic philosophy in their writings. Tieck thought that Nature lived like a person and would one day declare herself to him. "O holde Natur, wie beutst du mir heut wieder die Wange zum zärtlichsten Kuß, wie fühl' ich deinen reinen Atem, und in deiner Umarmung dein treues freundliches Gemüt!" [95] In descriptions of landscape Tieck shows an interesting kinship with Giraudoux. Compare the following passages with their remarkable verbs:

Die Nacht tritt ernst und feierlich herauf, die schwarzen Heere von Wolken ziehen unter Sternenglanz auf und ab. ... Bäume wachsen hervor, die er nicht kennt, sie scheinen zu reden und menschlichen Sinn und Liebe und Vertrauen gegen ihn auszudrücken. ...

---

[92] *Provinciales* (Grasset, 1922), p. 64.
[93] *Athenaeum,* III, 96.
[94] *Ondine,* Act II, sc. 11.
[95] "Phantasus," *Deutsche Literatur,* ser. 17, vol. IV, p. 268.

Die Büsche flüstern ihm liebe Worte ins Ohr, wenn er vorübergeht, fromme Lämmer drängen sich um ihn, die Quelle scheint ihn mit lockendem Murmeln mit sich führen zu wollen, das Gras unter seiner Füßen quillt frischer und grüner hervor.[96]

Un arbre poussa tout à coup à côté de ma table, me meurtrissant le bras, et, soudain, comme je ne les avais jamais vus, tous les arbres se dressèrent dans la campagne et avancèrent vers nous; les peupliers, par escouades de trois, qu'on ne devait pas séparer, même sur les navires; des chapelets d'aulne au pied desquels serpentait un ruisseau d'ombre presque tari; un pin parasol, qui abaissait ses branches comme un marchepied et d'où l'ombre descendait, noblement; puis les acacias que la foudre épargne, car chaque feuille a son paratonnerre. Puis la Forêt, laissant les clairières comme traces de ses pas.[97]

As nature is characteristically endowed with human attributes, so the human personality melts into the great indefinable streams of nature. The key to Novalis' cosmology lies in his statement: "Der Mensch ist eine Analogienquelle für das Weltall." Through symbolism and analogy he unifies all nature:

Ich würde meinen Sinn oder Körper teils durch sich selbst, teils durch die *Idee* des Ganzen—durch seinen Geist—die Weltseele bestimmt finden und zwar beides als unzertrennlich vereinigt, sodaß man genau weder das eine noch das andre ausschließend sagen könnte. Mein Körper würde mir nicht spezifisch von Ganzen verschieden—sondern nur als eine Variation desselben vorkommen. Meine Erkenntnis des Ganzen würde also den Charakter der Analogie haben.[98]

Romantic authors attempt to restore to personality the same fluidity which it possessed in the *Märchen* by depicting characters which escape the conventional moulds. Tieck and Hoffmann permit their characters to slip entirely out of the human condition. Giraudoux's creatures change into mermaids or gods.

A less extravagant means of cracking the brittle integrity of personality may be observed in the frequent cases of split personality. *Die Elixiere des Teufels* offers a particularly interesting example. Also, in Tieck's plays, characters split into several others. The *Doppelgänger* and the *golems* of German literature are reflected in Giraudoux's *sosies*. The case of Jacques Forestier alias Siegfried von Kleist places directly before us this problem of psychological ambiguity. In *Amphitryon* and *Judith* a mainspring of dramatic action is the confusion of identities. There is a false Amphitryon (Jupiter) and a false Holophernes (Egon) to bewilder the heroines and complicate the plots. Amphitryon's servant is doubled by Mercury, and Judith herself has an *alter ego* in Suzanne. In the latter play the drunken guard is an angel. Everywhere the spirit of the masked ball pervades the work of Jean Giraudoux. The false parents of Ondine are the real parents of Bertha. Orestes plays a double rôle, that of the "stranger" and the brother and son. Disguise, substitution, double and imprecise identity keep personality in a constant state of flux.

Giraudoux conceives of personality as subject to continual transformation. It may undergo a series of progressive mutations. In the case of Brossard (*Combat avec*

[96] "Wundersame Liebesgeschichte der schönen Magelone und des Grafen Peter aus der Provence," *ibid.*, II, 283.

[97] *Provinciales*, p. 88.

[98] *Op. cit.*, II, 340–41.

*l'Ange*), we witness five or six "éclusages." At each level, the president's nature is subjected to a complete alteration. Giraudoux's characters typically assume rôles for a time and then reject them, like creatures shedding their skins. Bardini flees from the rôle he has held as a model husband and father; Edmée likewise breaks the image she has made of herself. They are as if constantly in search of an elusive identity. When they find their nature, however, they are no more human beings, but dead abstractions. They would have preferred anonymity. Giraudoux's tragic characters are those whose personal identities have become fixed.

In the French novel the personages are characteristically static, permanently situated in relation to the dramatic problem which the author treats. The malleability of the Giralducian hero places him more in the German tradition. Heinrich von Ofterdingen and Sternbald possess an extraordinary capacity for alteration and transformation. The German characters are subject to such constant shifting that they seem without any precise identity at all. They are utterly passive, subject to higher forces as great and mysterious as those which move the tides. One is not surprised to read that Tieck wrote Solger that he had been enormously impressed by Hume's notion according to which the soul is only the reflection of diverse appearances which succeed one another in the flood of time.[99]

Tieck sums up the German position by placing the human personality under the law of the everlasting *Werdende:* everything changes, nothing remains; we exist only because we constantly change, and we cannot understand how an immobile existence could still be called existence.[100] Novalis states the aspiration of the Romantic soul: "Wir sind gar nicht Ich,—wir können und sollen aber Ich werden. . . ."[101] This lifelong adventure of the personality in search of itself defines the Romantic career. When Sternbald analyzed his feelings, Tieck tells us:

Wenn er so in sein bewegtes Gemüt sah, so war es, als wenn er in einen unergründlichen Strudel hinabschaute, wo Woge an Woge drängt und schäumt, und man doch keine Welle sondern kann, wo alle Fluten sich verwirren und trennen, und immer wieder durcheinanderwirbeln, ohne Stillstand, ohne Ruhe, wo dieselbe Melodie sich immer wiederholt, und doch immer neue Abwechselung ertönt: kein Stillstand, keine Bewegung, ein rauschendes, tosendes Rätsel, eine endlose, endlose Wut des erzürnten, stürzenden Elements.[102]

## Language

In the language of primitive man, Romantics found the source of all poetic expression.[103] Language had not developed into the dry sterile organ which civilization was to create for the exchange of ideas. It was fresh and abundant in images. Innocent of all conceptual knowledge, man instinctively expressed his reactions in

[99] *Nachgelassene Schriften und Briefwechsel hrsg. von L. Tieck und Fr. v. Raumer,* 2 vols. (Leipzig, 1826). Cited by Huch, *op. cit.,* I, 130.

[100] *Tiecks Schriften* (Berlin, 1828–1854), XXII, 120.

[101] *Op. cit.,* III, 122.

[102] *Franz Sternbalds Wanderungen* (*Deutsche Literatur,* ser. 17, vol. VI, p. 257).

[103] One will recall in this connection the great interest that the German Romanticists took in philological research.

terms of concrete objects. Nature offered him a treasury of symbols and signs from which he could illustrate his thought. In such close cleavage with nature, he remained sensitive to the harmonies and analogies in nature. He had not yet lost sight of the sublime unity of all phenomena nor been obliged to manufacture an artificial order which he will later try to apply to the world. He could perceive the true ties which link all beings. Nothing appeared to him isolated. His sense perceptions took the form of vivid imagery. His thinking was exclusively metaphorical. He delighted in bringing together things which were apparently the most disparate: now stars seem to him men, now men seem to him stars; stones seem animals; clouds, plants. "Er spielt mit den Kräften und Erscheinungen, er wußte, wo und wie er dies und jenes finden, und erscheinen lassen konnte, und griff so selbst in den Saiten nach Tönen und Gängen umher." [104]

To reaffirm the poetic verities of the world, Romantics could find no better way than to return to the *Bildersprache* of early man. Hoffmann preached that the metaphorical language of the poet, the child, and primitive man possessed a reality which is lost in the transition from unconsciousness to consciousness. This reality is, however, eternally true, and must be recaptured for mankind.[105] Among the German writers, Jean Paul seems to be most ardently in pursuit of this reality. In the magic of Richter's style, objects spring from their usual place to rejoin a distant likeness. By the slender threads of analogy he binds together before our startled eyes the most remote things in nature. His work presents a vast metaphorical tapestry of intricate pattern and rich color. What appears in him a particular gift, a vision, Richter would make a fundamental of literature. In the school that he founded in 1790 at Schwarzenbach he taught the art of writing by accustoming his pupils to grasp parallels taken from vastly different fields and to discover them themselves.[106]

Jean Giraudoux is one of the most accomplished of Jean Paul's pupils. No writer has demonstrated more faith in the magical property of the metaphor or abandoned himself more completely to its authority. It is the alpha and omega of his art. In the improvisation, which is his sole manner of composition, he allows himself to be led where his wit and imagination will take him. One image calls up another, which in turn provokes another; clusters of imagery form and dissolve before others. A word, a glance, a sound, the slightest impulsion suffices to set the process in motion whereby he creates the most dense and intricate metaphorical patterns. Every object or idea which arises in his consciousness seems capable of evoking a wealth of imagery, reflections in far distant fields. His pen never falters before a comparison, however incongruous, however remote the terms may appear to common sense.

His pen animates and transfigures all in its course. Elements fly from their conventional position and rejoin far distant ones whose affinity is miraculously exposed. Barriers which human industry has erected between phenomena, between the moral

---

[104] Novalis, *Kleine Schriften* (Aubier, 1947), p. 182. (What Novalis says here about the "master" represents well the Romantic conception of the processes of primitive man.)

[105] See *Der goldene Topf*.

[106] *Die unsichtbare Loge*.

and the physical, are suddenly breached. The accepted order is shattered and the elements of the world as we know it scatter and regroup anew. It is as if out of chaos the world were restored to its original order and brilliance. Giraudoux invites us to behold "les meubles anciens du monde comme Adam les vit ... et les meubles modernes dans leur divinité." [107] The primitive analogies seem to reappear and point toward the essences behind all phenomena.

Giraudoux's achievement would appear to realize the loftiest of Romantic aspirations. By bringing together in a metaphor two distant objects, their essence is disengaged and removed to a realm of pure abstraction. The peculiar atmosphere which characterizes Giraudoux's work is created through this process. Høst describes it as the impression of an added dimension.[108] One senses that the essences are everywhere mingling promiscuously with phenomena. The invisible seems just as much present as the visible. Qualities, the significance of things, become as palpable as the things themselves and can even replace them: basins are filled, not with water, but with the past; [109] happiness flows in the veins instead of blood, etc. Thus, by the mechanism of the metaphor Giraudoux frees his perspective of material limitations to behold shining through a transparent universe the abstractions which provide its basic organization.

Is it possible, however, to identify this plane of abstraction to which Giraudoux so easily attains by the metaphor, with the absolute, so earnestly longed for by the Romanticists? One hesitates for several reasons before such an identification. It would be more than presumptuous to assume that Giraudoux had succeeded where everyone else had failed. Moreover, the absolute, as conceived by all the seekers of the *blaue Blume* from Novalis to Mallarmé, has never been more than an ideal, a vague object of *Schwärmerei,* always to be sought, but never to be attained. Its nature has never been more specifically described than as a sign pointing away from the mortal and temporal toward the eternal and the infinite. Giraudoux's ambition, his *Sehnsucht,* is as strong as any other's; his conception of the rôle of the poet just as lofty, of the act of creation just as mystic. But his human limitations prove just as great. In the vast harvest of metaphors in Giraudoux's work, many are on a level of high seriousness, but others amount to little more than verbal embroidery. Many figures reveal at most only a superficial analogy, images which have practical autonomy, do not illustrate anything. What affinity can be located seems merely an excuse to record another image. In this playful fortuity, this sort of self-parody, we can read the testimony of Giraudoux's limitations and the defeat he shares with all seekers of the absolute. It is called Romantic irony.

## Romantic irony

Irony is the natural corollary to an art of transcendental pretensions. It is born out of the poet's despair to rise above his human condition. He must mock his attempts

[107] *Juliette au pays des hommes,* p. 189.
[108] *Op. cit.,* Chapter XII.
[109] *Eglantine* (Grasset, 1927), p. 78.

to keep from suffering too greatly from his frustration. It is a means of reasserting his dignity, his mastery over himself and his work. The process of irony is a subtle device of manifold implication and significance. Let us examine some of its aspects in theory and practice as developed by the Romantic writers.

Romantic art is, in general, marked by a characteristic polarity. Effusions which rise spontaneously from the heart meet the sobering processes of the intellect. By Romantic definition the poet is a *possédé*. But at the height of his fervor common sense intervenes to cut short his transports. A sort of censor, defined by Friedrich Schlegel as the *unbedingte Willkür*, invokes the mechanism of Romantic irony. The poet becomes consciously aware of his inspiration and can regard its processes objectively and critically. However antipodal these two activities appear, they nevertheless operate so closely together that they may be considered aspects of the same thing. So Schlegel remarks that "Witz ist die Erscheinung, der äußre Blitz der Fantasie. Daher seine Göttlichkeit, und das Witzähnliche der Mystik." [110] Giraudoux states the same paradox: "Cette ironie ... dont l'autre nom est la poésie." [111] In their rebellion against intellectualism, Romantic poets never excluded all use of the intellect. They were opposed as much to one excess as the other. Both Novalis and Schlegel remark upon this point particularly. Exclusive use of the intellect leads to sterility, but unchecked inspiration would lead to childish babbling. Thus they maintain that a combination of the two is of highest necessity. To dream, and at the same time not to dream, is the synthesis which Novalis called the operation of genius.[112] The Germans were generally faithful to this principle. So, too, is Giraudoux. They always exercised some control over their *bateau ivre*.

Friedrich Schlegel, out of long reflection upon the relationship between the critical and creative faculties, established irony as a canon of the new *Dichtung*. He attached it to Fichte's doctrine of the sovereignty of the Free Spirit. This is the aspect which Ricarda Huch underlines in her definition:

Man könnte romantische Ironie am besten mit Geistesfreiheit übersetzen. Nicht naturlos, aber naturfrei ist der wahre Ironiker. Er hat die Fähigkeit, sich von dem irdischen Element, in dem er lebt und webt, zu lösen, als ein Luftschiffer emporzusteigen und die Erde als winzigen Punkt unter sich verschwinden zu sehen, die verhältnismäßige Nichtigkeit der lebenden Kugel zu erkennen, die, so lange sie fest unter seinen Füßen war, sich so breit machte und unermeßlich ausdehnte.[113]

The philosophic idea that the human spirit is superior to the facts of the universe, translated into esthetics, means that the artist is supreme over his creation. He is free to create it; he could have created something entirely different. It is his thing. He can play with it, amuse himself by seeing his own reflection in it, capriciously destroy it. Schiller had advanced a similar idea in defining the "Spieltrieb" in art.[114] Toward his creation, the artist is in much the same position as God toward the universe. He can imitate the processes of eternal creation and destruction which he observes in

[110] *Athenaeum*, III, 8.
[111] Preface to the French translation of Evelyn Waugh, *Diablerie* (Grasset, 1938), p. iv.
[112] *Schriften*, III, 34.
[113] *Op. cit.*, I, 279.
[114] *Briefe über die ästhetische Erziehung des Menschen*, Letter 15.

nature. Through the act of auto-destruction after auto-creation he exhibits the complete independence of the ego. He thereby evades the prison of his own construction, of his own assertions. Schlegel advised the artist to guard himself from losing himself too much in his work, as if there were danger of reducing thereby its value of expression. He must even be capable of renouncing creation altogether.

The exercise of irony is in a sense an act of modesty, an acknowledgment of human limitation. Friedrich Schlegel conceived of it as a constant self parody.[115] The artist must be able to dissociate himself from his work and judge with objectivity the child of his brain. He must always remember the precariousness of all affirmations and be willing to accept chaos. He must not be so presumptuous as to suppose he can contain the infinite richness of the living world, whether in its psychological or phenomenological aspects, in any formula. This is why in *Lucinde,* which represents sheer chaos in the novel, Julius praises chaos and expresses the wish that he were the son of Wit. Schlegel says: "Ironie ist klares Bewußtsein der ewigen Agilität des unendlich vollen Chaos." [116] The pirouettes by which Giraudoux escapes any commitment in his plays, a source of great vexation to critics who demand that an author take a position and remain consistent, may be explained and justified on such grounds.[117] Nature permits no arbitrary solutions. It is impossible for man to know the definitive truth about anything whatsoever. Irony is an expression of resignation before this metaphysical conviction.

The great bursts of hope and optimism characteristic of the Romantic mentality alternate with the bitter but philosophical realization that the world is chaos and life is illusion. Novalis admitted finding life just "eine schöne, genialische Täuschung, wie ein herrliches Schauspiel." [118] At such moments the poet masks his anguish by banter. As Fantasio tells Elsbeth in Alfred de Musset's comedy: "Qui sait? Un calembour console de bien des chagrins; et jouer avec les mots est un moyen comme un autre de jouer avec les pensées, les actions et les êtres." [119]

To interpret such mockery as evidence of superficiality or incorrigible puerility is to misunderstand completely. The very things Romantics take most seriously they bathe in this irony. In the *Athenaeum* Schlegel illustrates this point by the example of Goethe's treatment of Wilhelm Meister. Wilde has an aphorism somewhere about life being much too serious to be taken seriously. Romanticists consider it unseemly to sink too deeply into the tragedy of existence or to disdain pleasantry as nothing more than the privilege of children, unworthy of serious adults. Schlegel summarizes this Romantic form of stoicism thus: "Ironie ist die Form des Paradoxen. Paradox ist alles, was zugleich gut und groß ist." [120]

No one who has seen *Sodome et Gomorrhe* would question Giraudoux's capacity

---

[115] For Schlegel's teachings regarding irony, see Rudolf Haym, *Die Romantische Schule* (Berlin: Weidmannicke Buchhandlung, 1914), pp. 295–300.

[116] *Athenaeum,* III, 16.

[117] Mme Magny has an interesting discussion of the exasperating ambiguity of Giraudoux's plays. *Op. cit.,* pp. 95 ff.

[118] *Schriften,* II, 423.

[119] *Fantasio,* Act II, sc. 1.

[120] "Kritische Fragmente 48," *Deutsche Literatur,* ser. 22, vol. IV, p. 111.

for high seriousness. And a glance at the list of his works suffices to recall that he has
not avoided the great dilemmas of human existence. But in spite of his deep and
bitter meditation upon man's fate, he rarely lets a cry of anguish escape. His com-
posure and self-control are almost perfect. A dignified stoicism keeps him from
acting like a victim. His attitude toward the universe is that of a gentleman in the
presence of a boor: cool and slightly exaggerated politeness. That is how he himself
defines his much discussed preciosity: "de la politesse envers la création." [121] He
remains smiling and mundane before the greatest afflictions imposed upon mankind.
War, which preoccupies him so greatly, is treated with debonair courtesy, the defer-
ence one might pay to a person whom one hates, but fears to arouse. "Pardonne-moi,
ô guerre, de t'avoir,—toutes les fois où je l'ai pu,—caressée!" [122] Only when his
guard is down, does he let slip an utterance as balefully pessimistic as the war tirade
in *La Guerre de Troie:* "Si toutes les mères coupent l'index droit de leur
fils, les armées de l'univers se feront la guerre sans index. ... Et si elles lui coupent
la jambe droite, les armées seront unijambistes," etc.[123] No man who shows such
bitter hopelessness as in the above passage or who consistently expresses such fear
of destiny and suspicion of the gods can be thought of as a sunny optimist. His levity,
his superficiality is a deliberate attitude. It pleases him to give that impression.
"Giraudoux prétendait qu'il n'y a rien de plus puéril qu'un homme sérieux." [124]
"Je n'ai point tant de curiosité, ni d'ambition: je trouve assez d'épaisseur à la surface
du monde." [125] It is Giraudoux's way of asserting his dignity as a human being, his
"solidarity with his species." Through Alcmène he says: "Je sens trop mes fibres
continuer celles des autres hommes ... pour ne pas suivre leur sort." [126] Does not
Giraudoux confess somewhere that his besetting sin is pride? The humanity he represents has no need of pity. There are no sick, poor, or unhappy among his characters.
Alcmène, Edmée, Juliette are all perfect and thoroughly sterilized specimens. Only
in *Combat avec l'Ange* is there any suggestion that such a group might exist, and
the idea is introduced with the sole purpose of discrediting the sentiment of pity
in Maléna. *Jérôme Bardini* offers the same lesson in stoicism, a dry unbending attitude toward emotion and sentimentality. Let us not make the mistake, then, of
seeing Giraudoux's obstinate refusal to dwell upon life's miseries or ugliness as evidence of shallowness of character. His pretended indifference is part of a code, the
code of the Romantic stoics.

The devices employed in Romantic irony were not invented by the Romantics.
They exploited and systematized what they could already observe in Elizabethan
literature and in masters such as Sterne and Cervantes.

Incongruity is the basic element. Juxtaposition of the spiritual and the materialistic
produces the desired effect of cynical detachment. It protects against bombast and

---

[121] *Juliette au pays des hommes,* p. 230.
[122] Epigraph for *Adorable Clio* (Grasset, 1920).
[123] *La Guerre de Troie n'aura pas lieu,* Act I, sc. 3.
[124] Antoine Albalat, *Trente Ans de quartier latin* (Malfère, 1930), p. 108.
[125] *L'Ecole des indifférents,* p. 73.
[126] *Amphitryon 38,* Act II, sc. 2.

sentimentality. This is how we meet Gérard, Juliette's fiancé. He is sitting by a stream, daydreaming in the summer sun: "Il se trouvait sucer une paille,—et, jouissance exactement égale, il avait deux cent mille francs de rente. Il portait une ombre de merle sur le front, une ombre qui ouvrait le bec,—et pesée équivalente, sur toute l'âme, la silhouette d'une fiancée riche. ..." [127] Or a rhapsodical tirade ends abruptly in a joke. This is a common trick with Giraudoux the moment he discovers that he may have waxed too lyrical. A poetic reminiscence will begin: "C'était parfois la semaine où les acacias embaument. ..." Suddenly there is a shift to the comic: "Et nous les mangions dans les beignets. ..." We are prepared for the next: "Où les alouettes criblaient le ciel, et nous les mangions dans des pâtés." [128] The humor springs from the shock as the world of pure prose collides with that of poetry. The homely prosaic references which intrude into the idyllic or paradisical effectively break the poetic spell. Jean Paul shatters his prodigious sentimental effusions in the same way. He destroys the hyperboles he creates by self-mockery.

All the processes of Romantic irony tend to destroy the illusion of reality which normally sustains a work of art. What a Flaubert strived to maintain at all costs is precisely what Romantic irony undermines. The operation may be accomplished by the direct intervention of the author. He steps forward to remind the reader that the work is but an invention. Brentano, for example, pushed irony to its limits when in *Godwi* he permitted a character on his deathbed to refer to a previous page in the book! The atmosphere of tragedy and solemnity vanishes immediately. In the theater Tieck created the classic example in *Der gestiefelte Kater*. We hear the audience discussing the play. Any illusion into which the reader may have instinctively drifted is brutally dispelled. He is mystified intentionally, now presented with illusion for reality, now reality for illusion, jolted from one to the other until in complete befuddlement he is sure of nothing. He is left with the sentiment of complete chaos, which resembles for Romantics the real face of the cosmos.

Giraudoux frequently takes the astonished reader into his confidence and discusses his craft with him. The little play *Impromptu de Paris* is exclusively that. In *Juliette* he presents his secondary characters in a group and then announces candidly that he is now done with them. He confesses his tricks and exposes his technique.

The playwright Giraudoux reminds us by one means or another that we are seeing a play. Both in *Intermezzo* and *Electre,* we can observe the amusing phenomenon of characters telling unabashedly to the audience their function in the play. In *Intermezzo* the druggist announces that his business is to prepare the transitions. As the curtain falls on the first act of *Electre* the gardener steps out of his rôle to deliver a lamento frankly announced as not part of the acting. The play stops to permit him to address the audience directly, to tell them "ce que la pièce ne pourra vous dire." In *Visitations* Giraudoux explains that he uses the gardener as a mouthpiece for all the speeches too sentimental for the hero. The device is a compromise. Not willing to renounce "purple patches" of sentiment and rhetoric altogether, yet somewhat

---

[127] *Juliette au pays des hommes*, p. 10.
[128] *Suzanne et le Pacifique* (Emile-Paul, 1921), p. 3.

embarrassed by them, he relegates them to an irrelevant character and places them outside the play. By this subterfuge he protects his heroes and himself from the taint of bathos: "Tous les lamentos, les intermèdes passionnés, les couplets du coeur devant lesquels se dérobent mes vrais protagonistes, tout occupés à mener l'action au plus juste ou au plus vite, et aussi par pudeur de leur tendresse, c'est lui qui se les réserve. ..." [129]

Through the device of irony the poet bridges the gap which exists between the world of fancy and that of common sense. His restlessness will not let him remain long in one or the other. He is possessed of a dual citizenship and cannot easily decide the measure of his allegiance. The Romantic dilemma is exemplified in Hoffmann: "He seemed to achieve an unbridgeable dualism. . . . He led a double life and ever in his tales contrasted life as viewed from a merely rational standpoint with life as conceived by the romantic seer." [130]

This is the problem which Giraudoux never tires of posing in his writings. It may in fact be considered his principal theme. Beginning as early as *Siegfried et le Limousin,* we observe the opposition of the world of reason (France) and the world of poetic imagination (Old Germany). In *Intermezzo* on the edge of what is the most banal and humdrum of societies—a provincial town in France—Giraudoux describes a community of phantoms, a zone of enchantment. Isabelle, the young schoolmistress, is the only one privileged to cross the imaginary boundary separating these twin districts. Giraudoux's protagonists are all privileged in this respect. As they select either the path toward fancy or the path toward reality, Giraudoux demonstrates the implications of their choice. His plots amount to experiments with the problem. Jérôme Bardini and Edmée break with routine and commit themselves irrevocably to a life of poetry. Elpénor, the Kid, Claudie, Tessa incarnate this spirit of freedom. They have nothing to do with the prosaic world, and the law of gravity has no power over them. But the majority of Giraudoux's people, while eager to explore the fairyland, soberly wend their way back to reality. Suzanne sojourns on a magic island and finds no words too hard to express her scorn of Robinson Crusoe's pedestrian and homely virtues; yet she returns to marry a functionary. Juliette, too, returns from her wanderings to the prosy world of the province. Isabelle prefers the *contrôleur* to the specter. Their career reminds one of the man in Tieck's story *Die Freunde,* which by its proud acceptance of the human condition anticipates Giraudoux's "solidarity with his planet." Whatever temptations are put before the Giralducian protagonist, whatever ambitions he may have fondled, the humble world of ordinary mortal life usually claims his soul. In Giraudoux, as in Hoffmann, a healthy instinct brings him back to reality.

The above allusions to Tieck and Hoffmann indicate the choice which haunts Giraudoux's mind has been faced with varying degrees of anguish by every Romantic writer. But the Germans most typically elected the course of magic. Heinrich von

---

[129] *Visitations* (Ides et Calendes, 1948), p. 84.
[130] Oskar Walzel, *German Romanticism* (New York: Putnam's, 1932, translated by Alma Elise Lussky), pp. 248–49.

Ofterdingen will not make his father's mistake in interpreting his dream of the
*blaue Blume* as an exhortation to marry as soon as possible and settle down to a
bourgeois existence. *Sternbald* is a precipitated flight from the real. Even Hoffmann,
who was rooted more deeply in the exterior world than any of the others, leaves no
doubt as to his preference. *Der Goldene Topf* is constructed on a parallel of reality
and dream. Anselmus' happiness is his reward for the faith he has held in the dream.

But is Giraudoux's decision in favor of the mortal lot so different after all? His
reality has already undergone such a transfiguration that it resembles the magic
existence of the Germans far more than the everyday world we know. To return to
such a world is not much of a renunciation. Fundamentally they are all in agreement. The world of realism is a prison, but its existence, like that of other prisons,
effects an indispensable control over instincts which might otherwise get too far out
of hand.

### German Sources for Giraudoux's Theater

Except in connection with Romantic irony, no mention has yet been made of
Giraudoux's theater specifically and its relation to German Romanticism. Yet
several of his plays have German antecedents, and critics have more than once
evoked the German theater in analyzing a play of Giraudoux's.[131]

*Siegfried,* Giraudoux's first venture for the stage, remains of course the outstanding monument to his affiliations across the Rhine. That he should take up Germany
again as the subject of his first play indicates how deep was his interest, how much
the Old Germany symbolized for him a captivating philosophy of life. His aim,
one will remember, was "to regain contact with literary Germany." In dramatizing
the antithesis of the French and German mentality, the New and the Old Germany,
Giraudoux nostalgically harks back to a poetic land invented by the Romantics,
whose charm he would be pleased to see diffused abroad in the twentieth century.
All that Giraudoux found amiable in German Romanticism he brings forth in his
character Zelten, the soulmate of the Jena and Heidelberg poets: "Zelten avait
tous ces défauts superbes et voyants dont on ornait chez nous les Allemands jusqu'en
1870 ... il avait des cheveux blonds en boucles, il sacrifiait chaque minute de sa vie
à des chimères. ..."[132]

### Romantic dramaturgy

The transition from the novel to the theater did not alter Giraudoux's basic
literary and philosophic patterns which seem so suggestive of German Romanticism.
As a matter of fact, the affinity became even more apparent. *Intermezzo,* which
lacks the obvious signposts of German subject or German source (it is one of
Giraudoux's few original plots), was promptly identified with the Romantic tradi-

---

[131] See reviews of his plays, notably those of Lalou in the *Nouvelles littéraires;* Crémieux, in the
*Nouvelle Revue française;* also, in the *Nouvelles littéraires,* those of Martin du Gard, who alludes
to the German theater especially in connection with *Electre* (May 22, 1937).

[132] *Siegfried et le Limousin,* pp. 19–20.

tion. René Lalou described it as a German Romantic fantasy. Its bucolic setting, its prosy village characters, whose lives are disrupted by spookish occurrences, are elements readily recognizable as Romantic stock-in-trade. The play seems pervaded with a feeling of cosmic communication of mysterious forces operating which escape the *raison raisonnante*. But the strongest resemblance to German Romanticism, according to Lalou, lies "dans le but essentiel, la volonté de ne pas trahir la dualité de l'être humain en passant de l'inconscient au conscient." [133] The opposition between reason and intuition, a constant Romantic preoccupation, becomes a dramatic theme in Giraudoux's theater. Isabelle may be taken to represent symbolically poetic intuitiveness; the *contrôleur* stands for *raison ouverte* and the inspector is a caricature of *raison raisonnante*.

*Judith,* which may be Giraudoux's greatest play, was not a success. In trying to account for this failure, one should not overlook the possibility that the architecture of the play may have been vaguely disconcerting to French audiences. Benjamin Crémieux pointed out that *Judith* is built along German lines; that is, it is a history, a play of development (*Entwicklung*).[134] In departing from the formula for French tragedy, with the dramatic action situated at a point of psychological crisis, Giraudoux may have confused the public. A play without a crisis is likely to be too German for French taste.

With the exception, however, of *Judith,* Giraudoux's plays have been such popular successes that it is to them that he owes his greatest prestige. It is interesting to note his triumph in the light of the general failure of German Romanticism to produce successful plays. Historians of German literature attribute their failure to the same "flaws" which critics discovered in Giraudoux. His plays abound in structural faults, he cannot recognize dramatic situations, his attention to style makes him transgress laws of the theater, his plays are just fine writing, etc.[135] But the public gave little heed to critical mutterings and rushed to acclaim each new offering. The formless and extravagant plays of Arnim and Tieck, overflowing with whimsy, could not survive. It is too early, of course, to predict what Giraudoux's fate will be. But the enthusiastic popular response to his plays would appear to be a belated vindication of Romantic dramaturgy, which provides such an overwhelming place to lyricism and musicality at the expense of form and dramatic invention. His daring affront to Realism achieved a complete revolution in the French theater and gave it fresh impetus toward Romantic goals.

Giraudoux's dramaturgy adheres closely to the ideals set forth by the German school. He rejected the prevalent notion that the stage should offer social documents where the audience could see themselves faithfully represented in character and situation, completely reasonable, completely understandable. The word understand does not exist in the theater, we hear in the *Impromptu de Paris*.[136] "Ceux qui

---

[133] *Nouvelles littéraires,* March 4, 1933, p. 8.
[134] *Nouvelle Revue française,* XXXVII (1931), 970–74.
[135] See for example F. Porché's articles in the *Revue de Paris, passim.*
[136] *Impromptu de Paris* (Grasset, 1937), p. 82.

veulent comprendre au théâtre sont ceux qui ne comprennent pas le théâtre." It is hard to renounce citing whole pages of this play where Giraudoux offers so candidly his notions of the dramatic art and attacks with all the resources of his brilliant wit the shibboleth of understanding. "Le théâtre n'est pas un théorème mais un spectacle, pas une leçon, mais un filtre." The true theater belongs in the category of the church and of primitive magic: "Le théâtre, voyez-vous, c'est comme une messe de langage. Pas plus que la messe, il n'a besoin d'être minutieusement compris. Seulement il ne doit pas laisser tiédir la foi." [137] Style, language are its fundamentals. The dramatist, who is the prophet of his age, does not speak in the language of everyday, but in signs, signs of divination and incantation. "Car il n'est de théâtre que de divination." [138] Giraudoux's words recall so vividly those of August Wilhelm Schlegel that it seems scarcely coincidental. Our existence, Schlegel writes, rests on the inconceivable, and art must not try to solve completely the mystery. The people have kept a naïve and natural point of view: they do not try to seize all with the understanding. Hence the power of the church with its allegorical mysteries and the magic arts. The artist who will lift his audience above all earthly contingencies will do so by words and signs, "darf in der weißen Magie oder in der Kunst der Offenbarung durch Wort und Zeichen nicht unerfahren sein." [139]

## Giraudoux's plays and their German predecessors

Three of Giraudoux's plays have direct antecedents from the pen of German Romantic writers. *Ondine* is admittedly based upon the *Märchen* of La Motte-Fouqué; *Amphitryon* offers an interesting comparison with Kleist's play, and *Judith* with that of Hebbel. While they illustrate very obviously that Giraudoux continued to look to the Germans for models and inspiration, they are, of course, not textually faithful to the model or precursor as the case may be. A comparison between the Giraudoux play and the German one reveals diverse points of variation which isolate the distinctive qualities of each author.

The story of *Ondine* was recorded by an unknown author as early as the fourteenth century in a poem entitled *Der Ritter von Staufenberg*. La Motte-Fouqué created his charming *Märchen* from this legend of a water nymph who leaves her element and acquires a human soul through marriage to a mortal, only to be forced, through her husband's infidelity, to return to her own people. Fouqué's claim to fame rests upon this work, although its sentimentality and the numerous moral digressions may not appeal to the modern reader. He may be amused at the heavy bourgeois virtues and piety which Fouqué presents against a background of fairy-like irreality. The fisherman's hut is an altar to the homely German qualities of cleanliness, godliness, hospitality. We witness the very realistic preparations as

---

[137] André Rousseaux, "Entre le théâtre et le roman avec M. Jean Giraudoux," *Candide,* March 22, 1939, p. 6.

[138] *Visitations,* p. 128.

[139] Cited by Huch, *op. cit.,* I, 6. (Source not given.)

the nuptial chamber is made ready for the knight and the nymph. She who comes downstairs next morning is no longer an undine, but a *Hausfrau* who blushes in her modesty as she sets about her humdrum household chores. The lusty jokes at her expense make one forget that right behind the hut lies an enchanted forest!

Giraudoux, as one would expect, seizes upon these incongruities and develops them into delicious comedy. Thus he would have Ondine consenting to do the family ironing only on craggy peaks and recite her prayers only with her head under water. Contrary to Fouqué, he takes a wholly detached and ironic position vis-à-vis the old *Ritterstück*. From the first speeches of the knight upon the fisherman's threshold, the parody is apparent. Witty repartee, jests about knights-errant, pave the way for an hilarious burlesque of all the machinery of medieval romance. At times the play turns wholly to *blague,* revealing Giraudoux as an inveterate if charming prankster, thoroughly enjoying all sorts of caprices. He revels in talk of salamanders and quaint lore; in the last act he stages a medieval trial which wanders off into discussions of pastry. The second act especially is largely invention and completely Giraudoux. Dramatic exigencies necessitate abridgment of the narrative, which Giraudoux ingeniously accomplishes by the tricks of the illusionist who conjures up in a few moments the essential dramatic scenes which would normally take place during a period of ten years. Nothing could more effectively destroy the sense of reality or make it more fortuitous. The minor characters suggest variants in the plot. La Motte-Fouqué, obliged by the economy of the *Märchen,* also skipped over episodes. But his device is awkward and sentimental, falsely naïve. He explains that it would be too painful for him to dwell at length on the steps of the knight's gradual estrangement from Ondine and his growing fondness for Bertha.

Giraudoux's sophisticated and simplified version gains in conciseness and dramatic interest. Happily he chose not to avail himself of Fouqué's clumsy melodramatic device of the exposure of Bertha's identity. One will remember that Ondine, who has learned from Kühleborn that Bertha is the lost daughter of the fisherfolk, announces the fact before all the guests assembled to celebrate Bertha's name day. It is incredible that Ondine should think that Bertha would receive with pleasure the news of her social debasement. Giraudoux was wise in rejecting this scene which is so poorly motivated. However, one feels that Giraudoux's reason for trimming the German story is not so much dramatic expediency as it is to provide room for his arabesques.

Any stage version would, however, mean sacrifice of the voyages which are by far the best part of the Fouqué *Märchen*—the travels in the forest, terrifying with its wild scenery and its storms, menacing with its malicious earth spirits who worry the wayfarer, kobolds under the ground and water spirits led by the hateful Kühleborn who assumes a thousand disguises to trick human beings, and who has the most exasperating ability to change into a waterfall just when the indignant knight is ready to deal him his just punishment. The rescue scene in the forest when Ondine appears in time to save Bertha and Hans is enacted against a canvas of magnificent landscape and is the high point in the *Märchen*. The trip down the Donau to Vienna, which is one of the finest parts of the Fouqué narration, does not figure at all in the play.

In the case of *Judith* and *Amphitryon*, Giraudoux has created quite independent plays, and it would be improper to consider the works of Hebbel and Kleist as anything more than antecedents. While Giraudoux certainly was acquainted with the German versions, he owes them practically nothing.

Hebbel follows fairly closely the Biblical account. Judith is a widow selected by the Lord to destroy the enemy chief and save her people. She is little more than the means of accomplishing the divine intention. As such, she has not enough free-dom to develop into a character presenting the highest dramatic interest. She seems colorless and conventional compared to Giraudoux's heroine who sets her human will against that of heaven, shrieking her defiance even as she accomplishes her mission. She is a more tempestuous sister of Alcmène, but both struggle to re-tain their mortal status and reject their roles as women of destiny. In both plays Giraudoux utilizes an old legend to dramatize the situation which is so important to him, one which is presented again in *Electre*: man's sublime and futile rebel-lion against God. Judith symbolizes the cardinal sin of pride, which is another of his obsessions. In this play as in others, Giraudoux's appropriations amount to little more than the briefest outline of familiar plots which can serve as vehicles for his own problems and preoccupations. The free and godless existence of which Giraudoux never stopped dreaming he incarnated in Holophernes. He may well owe something here to Hebbel, who represented Holophernes as a philosopher and a joyous pagan who has to be told what the word sin means. Both authors give greater space to him than he occupies in the Old Testament story and make of him an engaging foe of the humorless, sin-ridden Jews.

In the matter of plot, Giraudoux's version of *Amphitryon* departs considerably from its predecessors. Kleist's play is admittedly based upon Molière's, which he follows almost scene by scene. He takes over all the comic scenes of the servant action, and even outdoes his model in slapstick and rough humor. Giraudoux omits them entirely and invents the Leda episode, more congenial to his taste for innuendo and sophisticated wit. However, both Giraudoux and Kleist shift the center of dramatic interest. Molière's play is a social comedy concerned with the problem of what is proper to assume in the face of wifely infidelity. With Kleist the problem becomes an intimate personal one. The role of Amphitryon is greatly reduced and Alcmène's moral crisis becomes all important. Kleist makes her the embodiment of true wifely love and devotion, but fails to make her virtue very appealing. She seems to cling rather stupidly to her principles although she was more moved by the honor which Jupiter paid her than Giraudoux's heroine. A suspicion of a false prude hangs over her character. Alcmène 38 is more sympathetic, in spite of her smug indifference to immortality, probably because of her cunning. Her ingenuity in devising means of duping the master of the universe, first by having Leda take her place, and then by offering friendship as a gift superior to love, save her from being a virtuous bore. Her failures and her successes are equally engaging and feminine. With Giraudoux, Alcmène carries the burden of the play, but her personal conflict, which is Kleist's theme, broadens into the more philosophic problem of the attitude of the human being toward the universe.

In the Kleist play the note of intimate tragedy is struck also in the portrait of Jupiter. Kleist's own experiences give poignancy to the loneliness of this character who futilely tries to associate with his inferiors on an equal footing: "Oh, Alkmene, without love, even Olympus is a desert!" Kleist, the genius and the aristocrat, is speaking from his heart when he describes Jupiter's longing to be loved for himself. Giraudoux follows ostensibly Kleist's conception of Jupiter, but without the anguish of the German. His Jupiter says: "Un dieu aussi peut se plaire à être aimé pour lui-même." The melancholy utterance of Kleist has turned into a petulant retort.  There is little Olympic grandeur about the fatuous Jupiter of Giraudoux's piece.

It is not necessary to pursue an exhaustive comparison of these plays. They are all in the common domain. We have observed that Giraudoux borrowed little more than the briefest outline and permitted himself all license of interpretation. Plot, with him, has little significance other than that of a frame to contain his poetic fabrications. The characters, whatever their original nature, discuss the problems dear to him and in a language which is his alone. The fact that he selected his material from German Romanticism indicates only what we knew already—his orientation and his familiarity with the German masters. A more important consideration is the question of spiritual affinity. Yet the differences between the Giralducian point of view and that of La Motte-Fouqué, Hebbel, and Kleist are certainly more apparent than their occasional similarities. There can be little question of imitation with a spirit as original as that of Jean Giraudoux.

### CONCLUSION

Giraudoux's relation to the Romantic school is that of a fulfillment of their theory rather than that of an imitator of their works. Aside from the obvious fact that Giraudoux is too original a genius to borrow extensively, the explanation lies partly in the nature of the school. Although enormously rich in theories, the German Romantic school is comparatively poor in works. Creative works remained experimental, frequently mere demonstrations of principles. Too, the Germans could never completely extricate themselves from the Realism of their time. From Jean Paul to Hoffmann, their works reveal a discrepancy between theory and practice. Giraudoux knew how, better than they themselves, to turn their teachings to account, and create an art true to Romantic specifications.

This first chapter has explored and attempted to define Giraudoux's relationship to German Romanticism. We have observed that through his studies in German he discovered an esthetic which he enthusiastically made the basis of his own art and offered as an antidote for the excesses of Realism and Naturalism. Giraudoux,  the poet who declared he possessed a Franco-German soul, is typical of the twentieth-century French writer who has enriched his own national literature by adapting to his own use the doctrines and values he has found abroad. A detailed research into matters of composition, style, esthetic objectives, has sought to demonstrate that there is not only evidence of close parallels, but that his work represents a realization of Romantic theory as formulated by the Germans.

Nothing could better show the danger of classification on a national basis. While exemplifying the German Romantic ideal, Giraudoux is nonetheless French. There is no disagreement with those who see in Giraudoux the exquisite flower of French culture. On the one hand, the history of French literature is too diversified not to offer a hundred precursors; on the other, his inspiration harmonizes perfectly with his native inclination. To those who might conclude from Giraudoux's lifelong preoccupation with Germany and the stamp that country bears on his work that he belongs exclusively in the German tradition, one should recall that the German tradition began with Rousseau! The spiritual family to which Giraudoux belongs passes easily over national boundaries. If he was particularly inclined toward the Germans, it was because he found in them ready-made a clear expression, an articulation of the principles which he recognized as his own and which he felt should prevail in France.

CHAPTER TWO

# The Surrealists

"Mais l'écriture automate bientôt lui fit concurrence." This phrase uttered by an able critic of Jean Giraudoux [1] suggests that in Surrealism, even more than in Giraudoux, we can observe the full flowering of German Romantic theories. Here, in the most significant artistic movement of the between-wars period in France, we see not only general endorsement of the Romantic ideal, but the esthetic practice pushed to its ultimate conclusion. "Les romantiques allemands ont ouvert un nouveau domaine que les Surréalistes exploreront avec amour." [2] Aragon, Breton, and other leading figures of the group acknowledge the affinity between their program and the Germans', and reserve for them space in their gallery of ancestor portraits. André Breton was the first to bring to light the peculiar genius of Achim von Arnim, and grant him the rank he merits in the history of literature and ideas. Breton's admiration for Arnim was a personal bond between the two schools, a point of contact which has persisted throughout the entire career of Surrealism.

Surrealism did not, however, as in the case of Giraudoux, owe its initial orientation to German inspiration. [3] Its origins are chiefly in the reaction and revolution born out of the chaos following the first World War. Surrealists chose their forefathers deliberately, to give reinforcement and precedence to their ideas. By adopting Gérard de Nerval as patron, they forged, however, an historical link with German Romanticism and established a sort of genealogy. The absence of direct influence makes the close parallels which exist between the two schools appear all the more remarkable. In reviewing the main points of Surrealism, we are struck by their proximity to the fundamental theories of the German Romantics. French writers of the twenties and thirties renewed the pledges made by the Germans over a century earlier, and took up, as it were, where the others left off.

### THE SURREALIST REVOLT AGAINST CONVENTIONAL VALUES

The great originality of the Romantic movement in Germany had been the breadth of its aspirations, its extra-literary aims. From this moment on, literature

---

[1] A. M. Petitjean, "Electre et Giraudoux," *Nouvelle Revue française*, XLIX (1937), 482.

[2] M. Nadeau, *Histoire du Surréalisme* (Ed. du Seuil, 1945), p. 61.

[3] Commenting upon Béguin's *L'Ame romantique et le rêve*, a reviewer concludes: "Ainsi les romantiques français, les symbolistes, et les surréalistes sont envisagés en égard à leur ressemblance avec les romantiques allemands dont ils ont à peu près complètement ignoré l'oeuvre et l'existence." *Revue de littérature comparée*, XVIII (1938), 577. And Anna Balakian quotes from the first inquiry conducted by the *Cahiers du Sud* to prove the little direct influence the Germans have had upon French poetry. (*Literary Origins of Surrealism*, New York: King's Crown Press, 1947, p. 22.) However, while it is generally admitted that there is little question of Surrealist debt to German Romanticism, the affinities between the two movements seem far greater than the differences that Miss Balakian establishes in her very interesting study. (See particularly Chapter II.)

has refused to remain a modest art or craft, content to awaken or express emotions. It arose to affirm a principle and a way of life. Literature is philosophy, philosophy is literature, Romanticists had asserted. Writers of Giraudoux's generation continued the push beyond the narrow confines of literature proper. With Surrealism, the fields touched or claimed by the others are completely invaded and explored. The absolute, all-embracing character of Romantic aspirations is reaffirmed. Surrealism claimed to be more than a poetic movement, more than an artistic revolution, even more than a philosophy. It entered all aspects of life, claimed to be a whole, a living whole.

## Anti-rationalism, anti-realism

The origins of Surrealism lie in revolt against the same spirit of rationalism and traditionalism which had occasioned the two other movements we have studied. The restlessness which Giraudoux described as smoldering in the generation of 1910 took on in the years following the war the proportions of a great incendiary. Now literary and ideological problems were rendered exasperatingly acute by the addition of social and moral considerations. Fed by the bitter disillusions of the war, the urge to break with prevalent institutions seethed into total revolution. Dada burst forth as the supreme negation of everything which had gone before.

Never before had writers attacked on such a broad front. M. Jean Cassou testifies to the complete loss of faith in any of the values and standards to which western civilization had adhered:

Certains jeunes gens sentirent alors plus vivement qu'aucune autre génération leur désaccord avec la vie; et le monde, non plus, ne paraissait pouvoir se penser lui-même. Rien de ses injustices sociales, de ses désordres, de ses absurdités, ni le partage de cette guerre, ses raisons et ses fins ne semblaient devoir dégager une règle, illuminer une adhésion.[4]

Dada's fury of devastation is so great that the others seem in comparison timid reformers. The difference is only one of degree and emotional intensity, however. They are all united in their effort to overthrow the spirit of rationalism and discredit conventional notions based upon common sense and logic and ossified into tradition. The Dada assault had been prepared for by the undermining of Giraudoux and others who resemble the German foes of the *Aufklärung*.

When Dada consumed itself in its frenzy, Surrealism carried on the fight throughout the entire between-wars period. Opposition to the discursive intelligence is inherent in the conception and development of this school born upon the ashes of Dada. André Breton called for the relinquishment of all control exercised by reason. In magazines such as *La Revue surréaliste* and in the several manifestos, reason was persistently harassed and denounced. Surrealists repeated that nothing very great can be expected from the mind, a statement they attributed to Hegel. Like Giraudoux, they were looking across the Rhine for the antidote which would combat the evil of French rationalism. Through Hegel they established contact

[4] Jean Cassou, Preface to Tristan Tzara, *Morceaux choisis* (Bordas, 1947), p. 9.

with Romantic doctrines, and styled themselves tributaries of German thought:

Nous pouvons dire que c'est avant tout dans la philosophie de langue allemande que nous avons découvert le seul antidote efficace contre le rationalisme positiviste qui continue ici à exercer ses ravages. ... Aujourd'hui comme hier, c'est au rationalisme positiviste que nous continuons à en avoir. C'est lui qu'intellectuellement nous avons combattu, que nous combattrons encore comme *l'ennemi dans notre propre pays.*[5]

### Clamor for liberty

Fichte's theory of the liberty of the ego had given the German Romantics the excuse to exalt above all else originality and individuality. Whereas rationalism tended toward conformity and discipline, Romanticism put no limits to the freedom of the individual. Surrealism insisted upon the same rights. Liberty, Breton announced in the first Manifesto (1924), is the only word which can be exalting: "Je le crois propre à entretenir, indéfiniment, le vieux fanatisme humain. Il répond sans doute à ma seule aspiration légitime. ..."[6] In the name of the rights of the individual, Surrealism called upon heads of mental hospitals to release their patients!

Nous n'admettons pas qu'on entrave le libre développement d'un délire aussi légitime, aussi logique que toute autre succession d'idées ou d'actes humains. La répression des réactions antisociales est aussi chimérique qu'inacceptable en son principe. Tous les actes individuels sont antisociaux. Les fous sont les victimes individuelles par excellence de la dictature sociale; au nom de cette individualité qui est le propre de l'homme, nous réclamons qu'on libère ces forçats de la sensibilité. ...[7]

*Nadja,* a masterpiece of Surrealism, begins with searching reflections upon the qualities of an individual which make him separate from all others, the nature of each man's uniqueness. The isolation and exploitation of this uniqueness is among the foremost aims of Surrealism. It can tolerate no restraint.

Nothing can hinder man's freedom more than to accept the yoke of a profession or career. Surrealists, like Schlegel, formulated a condemnation of work in general and an apology of idleness: "Rien ne sert d'être vivant, s'il faut qu'on travaille."[8] Life is a matter of living, not earning a living, they declared, and they promptly quit as a group the studies or occupations in which they had been engaged previously. "«Perfection» c'est *paresse.*"[9] Friedrich Schlegel had written that idleness is the consummation of the science of life. For German Romanticists, idleness permitted the joys of contemplation, the flowering of the inner life. Novalis lifted it to a mystic plane where the ego could passively absorb the universe. For Sur-

---

[5] André Breton, "Discours au congrès des écrivains pour la défense de la culture." Text reproduced in M. Nadeau, *Documents surréalistes* (Ed. du Seuil, 1948), p. 298.

[6] *Id.,* "Premier Manifeste," *Les Manifestes du Surréalisme* (Sagittaire, 1946), p. 15.

[7] *Id.,* "Lettre aux médecins-chefs des asiles de fous," *La Révolution surréaliste,* III (April 15, 1925), 29.

[8] *Id., Nadja* (Gallimard, 1928), p. 74.

[9] Breton and Eluard, "Notes sur la poésie," *La Révolution surréaliste,* XII (December 15, 1929), 55.

realists it meant the opportunity to wander about, looking and listening, observing the spectacle of life which postwar Paris had to offer. Everywhere they were on the lookout for evidence of sentiments and emotions unspoiled by culture and civilization, fresh experiences. Breton's *Nadja* shows the aimless wandering and exploring to which the Surrealists were addicted. Like the strange heroine of the book, they preferred living in the street, "seul champ d'expérience valable, dans la rue, à portée d'intérrogation de tout être humain lancé sur une grande chimère." [10]

The liberation which the postwar revolution demanded was total and absolute: "l'affranchissement total de l'homme." Liberation from logic and all that it implies, liberation too from morality, religion, family which keep man a hapless prisoner. "Tous les moyens doivent être bons pour ruiner les idées de *famille,* de *patrie,* de *religion*." [11] Compared to statements such as this, the claims of the German Romantics for social emancipation seem mild enough. But even more than all this. Man is undertaking nothing less than his entire liberation from what we are wont to think of as the human condition. Dada closed the door to any possible adhesion, any affirmation. The idea of liberation with Surrealism, however, took a positive turn. It was soon observed that the demand for freedom implied certain assertions, certain articles of faith. Once the preliminary operations of razing were completed, the new school could begin to build. Enthusiastically it flung itself into a metaphysical adventure after the German pattern. The experience followed a course not unlike the three terms of the Fichtean dialectic of the infinite, namely the affirmation of the infinite, the aspiration to attain it, the impossibility of reaching it.[12]

## The Metaphysical Adventure

Beyond the circle of man's habitual activity, uncharted territories beckoned to the Surrealists. He must enlarge his domain, surpass himself. Convinced of man's latent potentialities for greater knowledge of himself and the universe, Surrealists exhorted him to forsake his circumscribed and erroneous notions and launch forth on a new voyage of discovery. Enough juggling with formulas, language games, etc! The problem is to find a guide for the mind lost in its own labyrinth.

Plus loin que ce que la science pourra jamais toucher, là où les faisceaux de la raison se brisent contre les nuages, ce labyrinthe existe, point central où convergent toutes les forces de l'être, les ultimes nervures de l'Esprit. Dans ce dédale de murailles mouvantes et toujours déplacées, hors de toutes les formes connues de pensée, notre esprit se meut, épiant ses mouvements les plus secrets et spontanés, ceux qui ont un caractère de révélation, cet air venu d'ailleurs, tombé de ciel.[13]

[10] Breton, *Nadja*, p. 151.

[11] *Id.*, "Second Manifeste," *Les Manifestes du Surréalisme,* p. 99.

[12] At a later stage Surrealism partly withdrew and rephrased its objectives. It might be noted here that any exposé of Surrealism cannot dispense with a chronological approach. Its history has been one of evolution and constant movement. Affirmations, denials, denunciations, and endorsements succeed one another with bewildering frequency and it is only by remembering time and circumstances that we can see many Surrealist utterances as anything but contradiction and discrepancy. Moreover, in spite of the elaborate, interminable ceremonies conducted over Sur-

Surrealism was possessed by the same urge to see beyond the veil, to penetrate into the mysteries, which characterize the other groups. They inherited the Romantic obsession of metaphysical problems and aimed at creating a new mysticism:

N'en doutez pas, ce sont les ennemis de l'ordre qui mettent en circulation ce philtre d'absolu. Ils le passent secrètement sous les yeux des gardiens, sous la forme de livres, de poèmes. ... Achetez, achetez la damnation de vote âme, vous allez enfin vous perdre, voici la machine à chavirer l'esprit.[14]

### The mystic rôle of poetry

Surrealism inherited, too, the same vocabulary drawn from literature. The new mysticism was to be based upon poetry. The metaphysical problem was to be worked by an esthetic solution. The word poetry, which Surrealism endowed with all the lofty and general significance it had first held for the German Romantics, could no longer be identified with the literary genre it conventionally designates. Tristan Tzara defined poetry as an attitude of mind:

Dénonçons au plus vite un malentendu qui prétendait classer la poésie sous la rubrique des *moyens d'expression*. La poésie qui ne se distingue des romans que par sa forme extérieure, la poésie qui exprime soit des idées, soit des sentiments, n'intéresse plus personne. Je lui oppose la poésie *activité de l'esprit*.[15]

The word became again a magic talisman and a slogan. It stood for liberation and all that is opposed to the dreaded and despised reason. It implied a way of life full of wonder and enchantment, spiritually in tune with the invisible forces of nature. Jean Paul Richter and Giraudoux lived in such an atmosphere. They "practiced" their poetry, as the first Manifesto of Surrealism will recommend: "Qu'on se donne seulement la peine de *pratiquer* la poésie. N'est-ce pas à nous, qui déjà en vivons, de chercher à faire prévaloir ce que nous tenons pour notre plus ample informé?"[16] Poetry supplanted science and speculation as a means of highest knowledge: "Si l'on recherche la signification originelle de la poésie, aujourd'hui dissimulée sous les mille oripeaux de la société, on constate qu'elle est le véritable souffle de l'homme, la source de toute connaissance. ..."[17] The key phrase of Surrealist ambition was written by Breton concerning the *Chants de Maldoror:* "On sait maintenant que la poésie doit mener quelque part." Such an assertion illustrates how greatly altered the word has become. It rules out the conventional notion of poetry as a finite art. "Il rôde actuellement par le monde quelques individus pour qui l'art, par exemple, a cessé d'être une fin."[18] Poetry is a probing instrument,

---

realism, resuscitation is always possible. M. Claude Mauriac, in his recent study, suggests that as a doctrine it may still be merely in its infantile babblings, with a long important career ahead. (*André Breton,* Flore, 1949, p. 211.)

[13] "Lettre aux recteurs des universités européennes," *La Révolution surréaliste,* III, 11.

[14] Louis Aragon, *Le Paysan de Paris* (Gallimard, 1926), p. 80.

[15] "Essai sur la situation de la poésie," *Le Surréalisme au service de la révolution,* IV, 15.

[16] Breton, "Premier Manifeste," *Les Manifestes du Surréalisme,* p. 35.

[17] Benjamin Péret, *Le Déshonneur des poètes.* Cited by Julien Gracq, *André Breton* (Corti, 1948), p. 121.

[18] Breton, *Les Pas perdus* (Gallimard, 1924), p. 184.

important not for itself, but for the epistemological revelations it can make. Breton kept careful watch to keep his disciples from serving purely esthetic ends, and never tired of reiterating that Surrealism aimed far beyond literature.[19]

The German Romantic program had been turned in the same direction. It had elevated poetry to the status of a cosmic approach and suggested that the universe could be solved esthetically. Both groups appear as instances of a "folie de la poésie," in the sense that one speaks of a "folie de la croix." It is not irrelevant that celebrated mystics are invoked in Surrealistic writing. Was not the poetic state conceived of in the same terms as apply to a state of grace or a religious trance?

German writers were valued by the Surrealists for the metaphysical inquiry to which they had dedicated their art. Breton could find in Arnim revelations concerning existence and human personality which anticipated his own. Arnim's *Märchen,* characterized by the dissolution of personality, the confusion of the animate and inanimate unseparated by the stout stanchions of reason, mystery and magic mingling with reality, offered the poetic interpretation of life which Surrealism was clamoring for: "Nous voulons, nous aurons «l'au-delà» de nos jours. Il suffit pour cela que nous n'écoutions que notre impatience et que nous demeurions, sans aucune réticence, aux ordres du merveilleux." [20]

### Imagination and the merveilleux

Imagination was called upon again to replace dethroned reason. "Nous vivons encore sous le règne de la logique. ... L'imagination est peut-être sur le point de reprendre ses droits." [21] It was the only guide acceptable to the young revolutionaries, who felt, if anything, it was not yet crazy enough. "Folle du logis!" they exclaimed. "Un logicien a cru par cette épithète qu'il voulait infamante jeter la suspicion sur elle, alors qu'elle est chez beaucoup trop peu «folle», trop raisonable encore." [22] Antonin Artaud exhorted people to leave their ideas, their logic, order, and Truth (with a capital T) and recognize the reign of the marvelous. "A travers les fentes d'une réalité désormais inviable, parle un monde volontairement sibyllin." [23] In imagination they put all their hopes of liberation and aspirations to break through to the mysteries which lie beyond objective reality. "La seule imagination me rend compte de ce qui *peut être,* et c'est assez pour lever un peu le terrible interdit." [24]

The power of the imagination over mind and matter is absolute. "Nature, elle nie tes règnes; choses, que lui importent vos propriétés?" [25] Truth becomes a rela-

---

[19] Paul Eluard echoes the master in writing that Surrealism was "un instrument de connaissance et par cela même un instrument aussi bien de conquête que de défense." (*Donner à voir,* Gallimard, 1939, p. 85.)

[20] Breton, "Pourquoi je prends la direction de la révolution surréaliste," *La Révolution surréaliste,* IV (July 15, 1925), 3.

[21] *Id.,* "Premier Manifeste," *Les Manifestes du Surréalisme,* pp. 22–23.

[22] Nadeau, *Histoire du Surréalisme,* pp. 83–84.

[23] Antonin Artaud, "A table," *La Révolution surréaliste,* III, 1.

[24] Breton, "Premier Manifeste," *Les Manifestes du Surréalisme,* p. 15.

[25] *Id.,* "Introduction au discours sur le peu de réalité," *Point du Jour* (Gallimard, 1934), p. 22.

tive affair. "*En réalité,* est-ce que je dors sur un lit de moelle de sureau? Assez! je ne sais pas: ce doit être vrai en quelque sorte puisque je le dis." [26] Through imagination, poetry takes on a veracity which escapes reason, and the poet finds himself in a superior domain where the marvelous is taken for granted.

The magic atmosphere of the *Märchen* pervades typically Surrealist works. *Nadja* shows that mysterious forces, unaccountable to common sense, govern persons and events. Nadja and the author seem to be living in a dream, obeying impulses which they cannot comprehend. Nadja possesses powers of prophecy and magnetism. Yet she is captive of a spell which the author unconsciously exercises. Are these real people or phantoms, one wonders, drawn together by inexplicable circumstances and coincidences? "J'ai pris du premier au dernier jour, Nadja pour un génie libre, quelque chose comme un de ces esprits de l'air que certaines pratiques de magie permettent momentanément de s'attacher, mais qu'il ne saurait être question de se soumettre." [27] With *Nadja* we are in the full *merveilleux* of Hoffmann or Arnim, whose characters slip back and forth between the zones of reality and hallucination. Aragon, in *Le Paysan de Paris,* speaks of having read of such wonders: "J'avais lu dans un gros livre allemand l'histoire de ces songeries, de ces séduisantes erreurs." [28] Slowly he began to realize their reality and their beauty. As he traces the steps of his conversion, he speaks for all the Surrealist seekers of the absolute. Certain objects took on peculiar mysterious charms for him, qualities which seemed metaphysic and revelatory: "Un objet se transfigurait à mes yeux." The world became for him completely transformed through the *merveilleux quotidien:* "... La mimique étrange de l'électroscope à feuilles d'or. O chapeaux hauts-de-formes! Vous avez eu pour moi toute une semaine le noir aspect d'un point d'interrogation." [29] "Toute la faune des imaginations, et leur végétation marine, comme par une chevelure d'ombre, se perd et se perpétue dans les zones mal éclairées de l'activité humaine. C'est là qu'apparaissent les grands phares spirituels. ..." [30] The magic of poetic intuition enabled him to integrate the infinite in the finite appearances of the world. "Puis, sans peine désormais, je me mis à découvrir le visage de l'infini sous les formes concrètes qui m'escortaient, marchant le long des allées de la terre." [31] "Je ressentais vivement l'espoir de toucher à une serrure de l'univers." [32] A slight deviation from the normal in sense impression or logical perception suffices to open the door to the marvelous. "La porte du mystère, une défaillance humaine l'ouvre, et nous voilà dans les royaumes de l'ombre." [33] Instead of being misprized, these abnormalities should be valued for their beauties and revelations. "Je ne veux plus me retenir des erreurs de mes doigts, des erreurs de mes yeux. Je sais maintenant qu'elles ne sont pas que des

[26] *Id.,* "Premier Manifeste," *Les Manifestes du Surréalisme,* p. 31.
[27] *Id., Nadja,* p. 148.
[28] Aragon, *op. cit.,* p. 140.
[29] *Ibid.,* pp. 141–42.
[30] *Ibid.,* p. 18.
[31] *Ibid.,* p. 142.
[32] *Ibid.,* p. 141.
[33] *Ibid.,* p. 18.

pièges grossiers, mais de curieux chemins vers un but que rien ne peut me révéler, qu'elles. ... Un faux pas, une syllable achoppée révèlent la pensée d'un homme. Il y a dans le trouble des lieux de semblables serrures qui ferment mal sur l'infini." [34]

Hallucination, hypnosis, hysteria were phenomena especially prized as pure poetic states. Recognizing that the discoveries of poetic thought had been made principally by men mad or partially mad, Surrealists pondered the relationship between poetry and insanity. They followed avidly the research of Sigmund Freud and predicted the immense possibilities of psychoanalysis. "La psychanalyse, méthode que j'estime et dont je pense qu'elle ne vise à rien moins qu'à expulser l'homme de lui-même. ..." [35] The Freudian technique became an integral part of Surrealism. By deliberately simulating mental derangement poets became their own subjects for analysis. They believed the precious state could be invoked through an act of the will and that they could retain the power to return to lucidity when so desired. Thus the revelations of the *merveilleux* could be obtained without jeopardizing one's health. Breton and Eluard conducted such experiments in *L'Immaculée Conception.*

### The unconscious

Identifying poetry with the nonrational manifestations of the human spirit, Surrealists, like the Germans, sought to exploit every psychic state uncensored by reason. They found that the dream and the unconscious state offered the ideal conditions. Asleep, man leads a perfectly free, poetic life, in intimate contact with nature. "Le procès de la connaissance n'étant plus à faire, l'intelligence n'entrant plus en ligne de compte, le rêve seul laisse à l'homme tous ses droits à la liberté." [36] These lines open the preface to the first number of the *Révolution surréaliste,* which amounts to an exaltation of the power of the dream. Here in the spontaneous welter of irrationality Surrealists sought to comprehend the meaning of life. Here in the *merveilleux,* they sought the "seule source de communication éternelle entre les hommes," [37] the very law of life. Surrealists and their sympathizers were urged to communicate their dreams for the intimations of surreality which they might contain.

Jean Paul Richter had thought of the dream as a state of cosmic communication whereby the soul could become receptive to the highest mysteries. Albert Béguin's choice of Richter's Dreams offers interesting evidence that the possibilities which Surrealists saw in the dream were already quite apparent to this early Romantic. In the dream, language is completely deviated from its conventional function and takes on new powers. Cassou remarks that both schools build their hopes upon the communications of language so modified.

«Tout le visible adhère à de l'invisible,» a écrit Novalis, «tout l'audible à de l'inaudible,

[34] *Ibid.*, pp. 13–18.
[35] Breton, *Nadja,* p. 31.
[36] J. A. Boiffard, P. Eluard, R. Vitrac, *La Révolution surréaliste,* I (December 1, 1924), 1.
[37] Breton, "La Grande Actualité poétique," *Minotaure,* VI (December, 1931), p. 61.

tout le sensible à du non-sensible. Sans doute tout ce qui peut être pensé adhère-t-il de même à ce qui ne peut pas être pensé.» Jamais ces communications du pensable avec l'impensable, qui sont le fondement même de l'idéalisme magique de Novalis, n'ont-elles été reconnues, et senties avec plus de désespérée vigueur que, de nos jours, par le surréalisme. [38]

### Automatic writing and the image

As the method par excellence to record the data of the unconscious available during somnolent moments, Surrealists practiced automatic writing, a process already known to the Germans. Through it, the poet can directly record the spontaneous expression of his soul, his trance in all its integrity. He makes no attempt to modify or control, merely unlocks the gates and lets come forth the everlasting waters of his inner self, carrying all his hidden or half-avowed hopes, hatreds, feelings, and desires. The most gifted and painstaking artist cannot equal the treasures of beauty and knowledge which are produced in this way. "Le merveilleux est toujours beau, n'importe quel merveilleux est beau, il n'y a même que le merveilleux qui soit beau." [39] Language which is obliged customarily to further the ends of logic by giving a false sense of simplicity and order is now utterly liberated. This is among the first axioms of the Surrealists. "Qu'est-ce qui me retient de brouiller l'ordre des mots, d'attenter de cette manière à l'existence toute apparente des choses! Le language peut et doit être arraché à son servage." [40] Only then can language be adequate to penetrate exteriority to reveal the real nature of things.

Automatic writing flows in an unceasing stream of imagery which reflects without distortion the soul and the universe. The chief business of the Surrealist school is to exploit the image. Louis Aragon stresses its importance: "Le vice appelé *Surréalisme* est l'emploi déréglé et passionel du stupéfiant *image,* ou plutôt de la provocation sans contrôle de l'image elle-même et pour ce qu'elle entraine dans le domaine de la représentation de perturbations imprévisibles et de métamorphoses. ..." [41] And Breton: "C'est du rapprochement en quelque sorte fortuit des deux termes qu'a jailli une lumière particulière, *lumière de l'image,* à laquelle nous nous montrons infiniment sensibles." [42] The supreme poetic achievement is the metaphor:

Comparer deux objets aussi éloignés que possible l'un de l'autre, ou, par toute autre méthode, les mettre en présence d'une manière brusque et saisissante, demeure la tâche la plus haute à laquelle la poésie puisse prétendre. Et cela doit tendre de plus en plus à s'exercer son pouvoir inégalable, unique, qui est de faire apparaître l'unité concrète des deux termes mis en rapport et de communiquer à chacun d'eux, quel qu'il soit, une vigueur qui lui manquait tant qu'il était pris isolément. Ce qu'il s'agit de briser, c'est l'opposition tout formelle de ces deux termes; ce dont il s'agit d'avoir raison, c'est de leur apparente disproportion qui ne tient qu'à l'idée imparfaite, infantile qu'on se fait de la nature, de l'extériorité du temps et de l'espace. Plus l'élément de dissemblance im-

[38] Jean Cassou, *Pour la poésie* (Corrêa, 1935), pp. 268–69.
[39] Breton, "Premier Manifeste," *Les Manifestes du Surréalisme,* p. 29.
[40] *Id.,* "Introduction au discours sur le peu de réalité," *Point du Jour,* p. 26.
[41] Aragon, *op. cit.,* p. 81.
[42] Breton, "Premier Manifeste," *Les Manifestes du Surréalisme,* p. 61.

médiate paraît fort, plus il doit être surmonté et nié. C'est toute la dignification [*sic*] de l'objet qui est en jeu.[43]

Produced by the unconscious, the Surrealist image replied to the German notion of the spontaneous image. Surrealists endorsed wholeheartedly the previous Romantic claims for such images. Images are a means of knowledge. They attain a *réalité suprême.*[44]

Le fantastique ou le merveilleux. C'est dans cette zone que ma connaissance était proprement la notion. J'y accédais par un escalier dérobé, l'image. La recherche abstraite me l'a fait tenir pour une illusion grossière et voici qu'à son terme la notion, dans sa forme concrète, avec son trésor de particularités, ne me semble plus en rien différente de ce mode méprisé de la connaissance, l'image qui est la connaissance poétique, et les formes vulgaires de la connaissance ne sont, sous le prétexte de la science ou de la logique, que les étapes conscientes que brûle merveilleusement l'image, le buisson ardent.[45]

The correspondences and analogies which they expose suggest the real cosmic structure and serve to establish an improved system of identification: "Car chaque image, à chaque coup, nous force à réviser tout l'Univers. Et il y a pour chaque homme une image à trouver qui anéantit tout l'Univers." [46] By means of the metaphor the unification of the universe is accomplished. Eluard cites the phrase of Lautréamont, also praised by Breton: "C'est un homme ou une pierre ou un arbre qui va commencer le quatrième chant." He matches it with two quotations from Novalis: "Hommes, bêtes, plantes, pierres et étoiles, éléments, sons, couleurs, apparaissent ensemble comme une seule famille, agissent et s'entretiennent comme UNE même race." "Henri d'Ofterdingen devient fleur, animal, pierre, étoile." [47] Pierre Reverdy said the image was the coming together of two realities. The farther they are away and the more exact their *rapprochement* the stronger their poetic reality.[48] The images produced in automatic writing offer the "révélation" which is for Breton necessary to beauty. "Une telle beauté ne pourra se dégager que du sentiment poignant de la chose révélée, que de la certitude intégrale procurée par l'éruption d'une solution qui, en raison de sa nature même, ne pouvait nous parvenir par les voies logiques ordinaires." [49]

Thus Surrealism offered once again the esthetic solution to the riddle of the universe. Here again we see poets turned theologians and metaphysicians.

## Integral Materialism

Once in possession of its principal procedures and settled in its basic position, Surrealism began to define its objectives more closely. The precedent of the German

---

[43] *Id., Les Vases communicants* (Cahiers Libres, 1932), p. 129.
[44] See C. Mauriac, *André Breton*, p. 206.
[45] Aragon, *op. cit.*, p. 246.
[46] *Ibid.*, p. 81.
[47] *Donner à voir*, pp. 73–74.
[48] Pierre Reverdy, *Nord-Sud*, March, 1918. (Cited in *Les Manifestes du Surréalisme*, p. 38.)
[49] *L'Amour fou* (Gallimard, 1937), pp. 20–21.

Romantics began to appear dangerous. Had their efforts to penetrate the mysteries of the universe through the rapt attention to the pulsation of their soul led them to any real victory? Had they actually been able to transcend the human condition? Breton and the others grew increasingly skeptical. Surrealism had arrived at the third step of the Fichtean dialectic, the sense of the impossibility of attaining infinity.

German Romanticism and French Symbolism appeared as tragic lessons on the frustration and defeat awaiting poets who dupe themselves by placing a too great transcendental value upon their revelations. The transformation of the world achieved through verbal magic looked to the Surrealists not so much as contact with the absolute as self-delusion and easy evasion. By spiritualizing the world, the Germans and the Symbolists had effected a poetic flight from life, but failed to solve its fundamental problems. Thus, led by the cult of the dream and the faith in the imagination to the very door of German idealism, Surrealists hesitated, then retreated from this path which appeared easy but fallacious refuge. "Il y allait, pour nous aussi, de la nécessité d'en finir avec l'idéalisme proprement dit!" [50]

Renouncing the "idealization" of the world, Breton hastened to affirm the "integral materialism" of poetry and tie it fast to reality. "Partis d'un idéalisme assez mystique de toute puissance de l'esprit sur la matière, les surréalistes aboutissent, du moins théoriquement, à un matérialisme de révolution dans les choses mêmes." [51] The Germans would henceforth be denounced as futile and false masters, "car ... ce ne sont pas ces 'rêveurs' qui brisent la prison où l'homme se débat. ... Ils s'en évadent par le haut." [52] Let the sick seek refuge in spirituality. Surrealists took their stand with life and set about to make poetry "une action directe au sein même d'un univers actuel." [53]

Breton's loyalty to Arnim, however, remained unshaken. He tried to justify it on the grounds of Arnim's firm adherence to reality. Nothing in Arnim, Breton wrote in his preface to the *Contes,* of the vagueness, the irresolution, the arbitrariness which characterizes Novalis. He subscribed to Hegel's judgment upon *Heinrich von Ofterdingen.* He translates from the *Jahrbücher für wissenschaftliche Kritik:*

Le jeune auteur s'est laissé entrainer par une première invention brillante, mais il n'a pas vu combien une pareille conception est défectueuse, précisément parce qu'elle est irréalisable. Les figures incorporelles et les situations creuses se dérobent sans cesse devant la réalité où elles devraient pourtant s'engager résolument si elles-mêmes prétendaient à quelque réalité. [54]

Hoffmann, who is usually considered among the Romantics to be the one giving most strongly a sense of reality, is pushed aside as a creator of "pacotille" devils. On the back of the cover of the catalogue of Surrealist publications, we find: "Lisez

---

[50] Breton, "Second Manifeste," *Les Manifestes du Surréalisme,* p. 116.
[51] Nadeau, *Histoire du Surréalisme,* p. 34.
[52] *Ibid.,* p. 61.
[53] Cassou, *Pour la poésie,* p. 297.
[54] Breton, Preface to the *Contes bizarres d'Achim von Arnim.* (Text reproduced in *Point du Jour,* p. 164.)

Arnim; ne lisez pas Hoffmann." Heine and Gautier have done Arnim injustice in describing him only as an author of terror stories,. His characters, Breton declared, behave with a naturalness not matched by any other of the German *conteurs*.

## *The everyday* merveilleux

The retreat from the path of idealism did not alter the basic methods of Surrealism. It meant chiefly that Surrealists would henceforth stress the scientific and demonstrative character of their experiments, and declare their positive contribution to man's general welfare. The magic of poetry, rejected as a means of cosmic contemplation, was made to serve humbler and more immediate tasks. The absolute which German idealism had sought behind phenomena in the mysterious regions of the world spirit or in God seemed to be centered in man himself, in his notion of things. "L'«idéal»n'est autre chose que le matériel transposé et traduit dans la tête des hommes." [55] The pursuit of the *merveilleux* would not stop. But it must not serve as an escape. It should be exhaustively studied as an integral part of life, as the key to man's relationships with nature, with the non-ego:

Au cours du développement du surréalisme se situera, hors de tout idéalisme, hors des rêvasseries des narcoses religieuses, ce merveilleux qui se fait jour dans le *réel,* le surnaturel, l'insolite, l'amour, le sommeil, l'hallucination, la sexualité et les troubles qu'elle engendre, la folie, les chimères, les prétendus désordres de tous genres, une rue comme toutes les autres, la poésie, le sang, le hasard, la peur, les évasions quelles qu'elles soient, les spectres, le loisir, les interprétations des rêves, l'empirisme, l'absurde, le conte à dormir debout, la surréalité.[56]

In analyzing the elements of the *merveilleux,* Surrealists were particularly struck by the singular rôle chance plays in life. Its mechanism seemed to contain the very secret of the *merveilleux.* This is the problem which Breton attacked in *Nadja.* In relating there the episodes of his life, he considered important only what lay outside of its organic plan, only "dans la mesure où elle est livrée aux hasards, au plus petit comme au plus grand, où elle se soustrait passagèrement à mon influence." He goes on to describe a world of mysterious encounters and coincidences:

Il s'agit de faits dont la valeur intrinsèque est des moins contrôlables mais qui, par leur caractère absolument inattendu, violemment incident, ... Il s'agit de faits qui peuvent être de l'ordre de la constatation pure mais qui présentent chaque fois toutes les apparences d'un signal, sans qu'on puisse dire au juste de quel signal, qui font qu'en pleine solitude je jouis encore d'invraisemblables complicités, qui me convainquent de mon illusion, lorsqu'il m'est arrivé quelque temps de me croire seul à la barre du navire.[57]

Like Giraudoux, Breton believes that objects can make signals to one, that daily life is full of little signs, a "forêt d'indices" to interpret. In some incomprehensible way the subjective and the objective worlds are connected. What is chance? Breton lists definitions from Aristotle to Freud and Engels, concluding with what he calls

[55] *Id.,* "Misère de la poésie. L'Affaire Aragon devant l'opinion publique." (Cited by Nadeau, *Documents surréalistes,* note to p. 214.)
[56] G. Hugnet, *Petite Anthologie poétique du Surréalisme* (J. Buchner, 1934), p. 14.
[57] Breton, *Nadja,* pp. 22–23.

*le hasard objectif:* "la recontre d'une causalité externe et d'une finalité interne."⁵⁸
Physical things, Breton declares, are capable of exerting strange magic powers over
man. He therefore surrounds himself with mandragora roots, statuettes, all the
paraphernalia of the *Märchen*. He suggests that articles on a table, furniture in a
room might even be arranged in such a way as to compel a certain person to appear.

*L'Amour fou* is devoted almost exclusively to pondering over marvelous hap-
penings.⁵⁹ What the *Märchen* presented forthrightly and not self-consciously is
here weighed down by the jargon of psychoanalysis and by farfetched reasoning.
Breton treats the phenomenon of prophecy as a projection of the human will or
desire into the material realm. He cites several examples such as his poem *Tournesol*
which depicts exactly an experience he was to have years after the poem was written and published.⁶⁰ Again, in trying to explain his great interest in a curious
spoon which he ran across in the Clignancourt flea market, Breton remembers that
he had once desired an ashtray in the fanciful shape of a slipper. The handle of the
spoon in question has a sort of pedestal in the shape of a shoe. Breton interprets his
discovery as the materialization of a wish.

Man's desire is that great force in nature capable of such miracles. Desire is what
links, as a "common denominator," the ego and the non-ego; it is the great unifying
element which transgresses normal causalities and "makes things come true." Desire, says Breton, "seul ressort du monde." German Romantics had understood the
capacity and strength of desire. It had become their catchword.⁶¹ Surrealists reminded people again that desire or love is after all the highest method of knowledge as well as the supreme escape.

*Love*

The importance Surrealists attached to the love instinct made it their principal
theme. They discussed and analyzed, conducted clinical investigations with testimony presented with scientific candor. No other literary school, not even the German Romantic, had given the subject such an importance. Freud taught them that
the basic motivation for all man's activities resided in the libido and that society
could do much harm by its suppressions and repressions. They rejoiced in this
further reason to attack existing conditions and advocated complete freedom for
this instinct which alone has the strength to reconcile man to the idea of life. The
Marquis de Sade became a martyr and a saint in the cult of *l'amour fou.*

The Romantic notion of the one and only love was examined with great interest

⁵⁸ *Id., L'Amour fou*, p. 32.
⁵⁹ But Breton is reticent about attributing to his revelation "metaphysical" significance: "De
notre temps parler de révélations est malheureusement s'exposer à être taxé de tendances
régressives: je précise donc qu'ici je ne prends aucunement ce mot dans son acception métaphysique mais que, seul, il me paraît assez fort pour traduire l'émotion sans égales qu'en ce
sens il m'a été donné d'éprouver." *Ibid.*, p. 61.
⁶⁰ Yet toward the end of the first Manifesto Breton wrote: "Certes, je ne crois pas à la vertu
prophétique de la parole surréaliste." *Les Manifestes du Surréalisme*, pp. 71–72.
⁶¹ Brandes, *Main Currents in Nineteenth Century Literature*, II, 27ff. (Kierkegaard exalted the
wish in *Enter-Ellen*.)

by the Surrealists. Nerval and Arnim, Breton wrote, illustrate "d'une manière saisissante le conflit qui va s'aggraver jusqu'à nous, l'esprit s'ingéniant à donner l'objet de l'amour pour un être *unique*." [62] While disapproving society's fostering of such an illusion for its "base ends," they accepted in principle the Romantic concept. It provided the godless with an acceptable mysticism, since its spirituality could be so closely identified with the carnal. A disciple of Breton writes: "Je crois à la possibilité pour une poignée d'hommes de faire entendre dans la seconde partie de ce siècle maudit le grand cri lyrique de l'amour et d'inaugurer un culte de la femme si profondément mystique et charnel qu'il fera pâlir à jamais l'étoile des troubadours." [63]

The erotic lyricism evident among the Surrealists is marked by a pathos more unusual in French poetry than in German. Jean Cassou, speaking of Eluard's *Capitale de la Douleur,* observes:

Là, on entrevoyait, à travers les démarches inextricables de cette poésie de rêve, une obsession amoureuse et douloureuse d'un caractère infiniment pathétique. Peut-être même y avait-il là l'indication d'un lyrisme érotique assez nouveau dans la poésie française—et que, je crois, on ne retrouverait que dans le masochisme de la poésie allemande—l'idée d'un servage passionné, d'une dépendance absolue, tragiquement absolue.[64]

André Breton saw in this common interest a bond between the two schools. He paid homage to German perspicacity in recognizing the association between art and the heart. "Ce n'est pas en effet la moindre gloire des romantiques que d'avoir pris conscience du fait que les vraies possibilités du génie artistique gisent seulement dans les ombres du coeur." [65] He himself is persuaded that poetry, for example, is in some way connected with the sexual instinct. In *L'Amour fou* he takes up in some detail the part of eroticism in art. Breton offers a curious testimony to the intimate relationship between the erotic emotion and the esthetic by confessing that in the presence of beauty in art or nature, he is seized by a feeling akin to erotic pleasure. This would account for his famous definition: "La beauté convulsive sera érotique-voilée. ..." [66]

### Integration and synthesis

Surrealists were satisfied that their recognition of the *merveilleux* and the magic of love was not incompatible with a "materialistic" conception of the world. The knowledge acquired through investigation in these fields was defended as conducive to a total comprehension of man, his reality and his relation with the universe. The insufficiencies of accredited sciences were glaringly apparent. Surrealism demanded further investigation in those fallen today in disrepute: astrology, the metapsychic, particularly cryptesthesia. The faith in the discursive intellect to the exclusion of all other faculties has given us a sadly limited notion of the world. In

[62] *L'Amour fou,* p. 10.
[63] Sarane Alexandrian, "Amour, révolte, et poésie," *Le Surréalisme en 1947,* p. 101.
[64] Cassou, *Pour la poésie,* p. 272.
[65] Breton, Preface to the *Contes bizarres d'Achim von Arnim.* (*Point du Jour,* p. 164.)
[66] *Id., L'Amour fou,* p. 26.

1942 Breton still mused over these problems. Man is probably not the center of the universe. There may be higher beings whose existence we cannot even recognize. He concludes with Novalis: "Nous vivons en réalité dans un animal dont nous sommes les parasites. La constitution de cet animal détermine la nôtre et vice-versa." [67] Occult sciences, esoteric practices must be taken into account. Their revelations of the *merveilleux* unify a universe divided by rationalism. "C'est comme si tout à coup la nuit profonde de l'existence humaine était percée, comme si la nécessité naturelle, consentant à ne faire qu'une avec la nécessité logique, toutes choses étaient livrées à la transparence totale, reliées par une chaîne de verre dont ne manquât pas un maillon." [68] The evidence Breton offers in *L'Amour fou* clarifies the whole problem of the subjective and the objective. And do not speak of illusion. Breton believed that he had hit upon "l'amorce d'un contact, entre tous éblouissant, de l'homme avec le monde des choses." [69]

Surrealists found in occultism the same pseudoscientific base for its speculations and assertions which had attracted the German Romantics. They presumed to revive the alchemist tradition and spoke of curious medieval experimenters like Nicolas Flamel. They were in search of the philosophers' stone which would permit man's imagination "de prendre sur toute chose une revanche éclatante." [70] Instead of trying to transcend the real, Surrealists sought to push back its boundaries. Surreality is not opposed to reality, but an aspect of reality—"une philosophie particulière de l'immanence d'après laquelle la surréalité serait contenue dans la réalité même." [71] The Surrealist objective developed as a great effort toward synthesis and harmony.

Surrealists were not unaware of the dangers involved in a complete abandonment to the irrational. The imagination can be just as treacherous a guide as reason. In spite of the frequent apologies of insanity and endorsement of the "dérèglement des sens" à la Rimbaud, Breton and the others hesitated to deny the other lucid half of life. In calling attention to the importance of the night they did not wish to exclude the day. Of what point are the manifestations of the unconscious if the intellect is not brought to bear for the sake of comprehension and conclusions? Breton scolded his school for not utilizing properly the data which offers itself in abundance. The value of automatic texts is their capacity to offer "des étendues *logiques* particulières, très précisément celles où jusqu'ici la faculté logique, exercée en tout et pour tout dans le conscient, n'agit pas." [72] The cooperation of the two faculties is indispensable for the success of any operation.

The basic quarrel with reason and logic was for erecting artificial walls between activities of the human spirit. Surrealists did not wish to commit the same error in the name of the unconscious. In place of such segregation Surrealists dreamed of

---

[67] *Id.*, "Prolégomènes," *Les Manifestes du Surréalisme*, p. 211.
[68] *Id.*, *L'Amour fou*, p. 60.
[69] *Ibid.*, p. 60.
[70] *Id.*, "Second Manifeste," *Les Manifestes du Surréalisme*, p. 165.
[71] See Cassou, *Pour la poésie*, p. 297.
[72] Breton, "Second Manifeste," *Les Manifestes du Surréalisme*, p. 141.

*(exact opposite)*

integrating the elements which had heretofore seemed antipodal. Breton defined the mission of Surrealism as a linking between the dissociated worlds of waking and sleeping, exterior and interior reality, reason and madness, etc.

Tout porte à croire qu'il existe un certain point de l'esprit d'où la vie et la mort, le réel et l'imaginaire, le passé et le futur, le communicable et l'incommunicable, le haut et le bas cessent d'être perçus contradictoirement. Or, c'est en vain qu'on chercherait à l'activité surréaliste un autre mobile que l'espoir de détermination de ce point.[73]

By a process akin to the Hegelian dialectic, Breton hopes to fuse two states into a new and higher one: "Je crois à la résolution future de ces deux états, en apparence si contradictoires, que sont le rêve et la réalité, en une sorte de réalité absolue, de *surréalité,* si l'on peut ainsi dire." [74] In 1934 he announced the progress already made toward the goal:

Le surréalisme, poursuivant son cours ... a provoqué des états de conscience nouveaux, renversé des murs derrière lesquels il passait pour immémorialement impossible de voir, il a—et cela on le lui accorde de plus en plus—modifié la sensibilité, qu'il a fait faire un pas décisif à l'unification de la personnalité, de cette personnalité qu'il avait trouvée en voie de plus en plus profonde dissociation.[75]

### Humour noir

To maintain a healthy balance, German poets had recourse to the device known as Romantic irony. Surrealists, fearful lest their surrender to the irrational might mean just exchanging one prison for another, were moved to create an emergency exit in *humour noir.* A variation of Romantic irony, it differs only in the emphasis it puts upon the macabre. This modern orientation is due particularly to the examples of Rimbaud and Lautréamont. Like the irony practiced by the Germans, *humour noir* results from the encounter of the poetic and the commonsensical. The same object which has been exalted poetically suddenly meets the gaze of cold lucidity. It is the "condition négative de la poésie." [76] A grotesque element has reduced the sublime—the poet's equilibrium is restored. The object has ceased to intimidate him, for he has shown his superiority. Such irony is never gay or joyous. It may be compared to a desperate effort to keep one's head above water.

In connection with German Romantics and Giraudoux we have indicated that irony often implies discouragement and defeat. The Germans, failing in their metaphysical ambitions, found comfort and dignity in mockery. *L'humour noir* is a product of the same frustration, but on an even larger scale. It is a sort of revenge on the world which will not be conquered.

Fundamentally, Surrealism was motivated by a profound despair. Man's attempts

[73] *Ibid.,* p. 92.

[74] *Id.,* "Premier Manifeste," *Les Manifestes du Surréalisme,* p. 28. Breton's own statement contradicts Francis Dumont's assertion that Surrealism considered the dream as the sole reality. "Ils ne voulaient plus, comme Baudelaire, concilier le rêve et la réalité." *Naissance du romantisme contemporain* (Ed. C.-L., 1942), p. 11.

[75] Breton, *Qu'est-ce que le Surréalisme?* (Brussels: R. Henriquez, 1934), pp. 26–27.

[76] Aragon, *Traité du style* (Gallimard, 1928), p. 138.

to find in religion, art, philosophy, science, a reason for living have all been illusory. The sum of knowledge which he has been accumulating during the centuries, instead of enriching him, has merely impeded his free movement. How can he reconcile himself to life? There remains love, but that is a solution for couples only! Hope is a false attitude of the mind, signifying nothing. All positive values must be rooted out of man's heart like evil weeds. Such is the extent to which the vital and aggressive pessimism of Surrealism could go. Of all solutions, humor is the only acceptable one. It is a solution because it denies all solutions.

Giraudoux cultivated a polite detached attitude toward his work and creation. The Germans preferred to make fun of themselves before anyone else could. Surrealism, intoxicated by examples such as Jarry, Vaché, etc., took perverse pleasure in vituperating sooner or later even the things which it had held in esteem.[77] It seems as if fear of being the dupe, even of themselves, made Surrealists keep constantly in mind the slogan M. Dumont suggests for them: "Ne rien prendre au sérieux. Pas même soi-même." [78]

The fact that no school of poets probably ever took itself more seriously is further testimony to the paradox of Surrealism. And all this negation and hopelessness implied, not precluded, the possibility of an ideal. Behind their proclamations of despair Surrealists held to a utopian dream of man's golden age, which brings to mind vividly the German *Sehnsucht* toward the primitive. Shining behind the Surrealist gloom, one can perceive this steady light. If man could only break through the prison he has created for himself to move freely with innocent senses in the dawn of a new day! This age of mud would then give place to an age of gold. Breton's anguish at the spectacle of modern man takes the form of a positive longing for the paradise which was lost.[79] Before man's fall from grace and the subsequent development of the logical intellect, his primitive faculties were an integrated whole, his powers of communication perfect. To Jean Duché, Breton declared that Surrealists suppose man originally in possession of certain keys which kept him in close communion with nature. Subsequently he lost them somehow and has been since trying keys which will not fit. The contact can be re-established only by "voies poétiques." The voice of Novalis is echoed in this longing for the completely unified personality. History, alas, has been but the record of man's slow degradation and estrangement from nature. But with routine and automatism broken, man may again obtain the freshness of vision which characterized primitive man. He may again be capable of marveling before the universe. It is at least what the Germans, Giraudoux, and the Surrealists all have earnestly desired.

The final synthesis at which Surrealism aimed is that of spirit and action. Charles Nodier, in the preface to *Smarra,* defined the poetic existence as resting equally upon the illusions of the waking and the sleeping life, the dream and action. He

---

[77] Rimbaud and Freud did not escape.
[78] *Op. cit.,* p. 17.
[79] Hence his eagerness to observe Voodoo and Hopi Indian magic in the United States.

himself participated too little to illustrate his ideal, but the Surrealists attempted
to obtain such an integration. It was not enough to transform the world through
verbal magic. Surrealism undertook to accomplish it in fact. At this step it leaves
the plane of theory and speculation and enters the world of physical combat. Henceforth, Surrealism will become a positive force socially and politically: poetry in the
service of the revolution:

Le poète à venir surmontera l'idée déprimante du divorce irréparable de l'action et du
rêve. ... Il maintiendra coûte que coûte en présence les deux termes du rapport humain
par la destruction duquel les conquêtes les plus précieuses deviendraient instantanément
lettre morte.[80]

### Poetry and action

It is not within the scope of the present study to follow in any detail Surrealism's
political adventure. But the transition from theory to action which we observe here
is not without precedents. Rather it would seem to be the step expected from all
anti-rational movements. Whereas the cultivators of the intellect tend toward more
and more abstraction (Paul Valéry, for example), and isolate themselves in the
serene air of the spirit, their opponents are drawn by their convictions irresistibly
down to the market. German Romanticism ended in a political movement known
as *Junges Deutschland*. There is a certain parallel in the course both schools took.
What of Giraudoux? His case is not clear. Works like *Bella* are obviously polemical.
Others are threaded with topical allusions. *Pleins Pouvoirs, Sans Pouvoirs* are essays
in political economy. But the claim that Giraudoux's entire work, including the
theater, is made up of thinly disguised pamphlets, seems greatly exaggerated. The
citizen Giraudoux and the poet are separate people. M. Yves Levy, who attempts
to fuse them, is not very convincing.[81] Giraudoux remains with the older German
Romanticists who did not "engage" their art.

Robineau: Mais cela va créer des obligations terribles aux auteurs?
Jouvet: Aux auteurs? Non. Ils n'en ont jamais eu qu'une: celle d'être des écrivains.[82]

Surrealists, on the contrary, struggled throughout their militant career to keep
from being just that. Breton never ceased protesting that the esthetic aspect of
Surrealism was only incidental, that poetry was at the service of knowledge and
action. In the declaration of January 27, 1925:

1. Nous n'avons rien à voir avec la littérature. Mais nous sommes très capables, au besoin,
de nous en servir comme tout le monde.

2. Le *surréalisme* n'est pas un moyen d'expression nouveau ou plus facile, ni même une
métaphysique de la poésie. ...

3. ... Le *surréalisme* n'est pas une forme poétique. ...[83]

[80] Breton, *Les Vases communicants*, p. 171.
[81] "Giraudoux et les problèmes sociaux," *Paru*, June, 1946, pp. 7–14.
[82] Giraudoux, *Impromptu de Paris* (Grasset, 1937), p. 139.
[83] Nadeau, *Documents surréalistes*, p. 42.

The fact remains, however, that in spite of their dogged efforts to treat life and art as an insoluble entity, one must admit that they succeeded better in modifying the latter than the former. "Si le surréalisme aboutit, malgré lui, à une magnifique explosion artistique, il mène aussi à un cul de sac idéologique." [84] And Surrealist "action" has always been marked by inconsistencies and hesitations. The "affaire Aragon" [85] indicated clearly that Surrealism never considered itself bound to its declarations. One of Breton's most recent statements almost approaches Giraudoux's: "Le seul devoir du poète, de l'artiste, est d'opposer un non irréductible à toutes les formules disciplinaires. L'ignoble mot d'«engagement,» qui a pris cours depuis la guerre, sue une servilité dont la poésie et l'art ont horreur." [86] It may be argued that Breton's refusal to commit art to a specific political end does not necessarily imply a divorce between art and action. But it is remarkable that only the most subtle distinctions prevent much of what Breton has said and done from appearing wholly inconsistent. It would possibly be better, instead of trying to make him consistent, to remind ourselves that consistency could not be considered very rightly among Surrealist objectives. But on the purely esthetic plane, their contribution has been the most significant event of the between-wars period. Exploitation of the data of the unconscious opened up a rich field heretofore neglected, and cast fresh light on the nature of poetry. On the basis of experimental evidence, Surrealists revaluated notions of art and the artist, and accomplished reforms advocated since German Romanticism.

## ESTHETIC THEORY

The Surrealist stand in matters of esthetic theory is indicated by the distinction Surrealists have established between poetry and literature. In championing poetry, they oppose all objective or conscious art, which they contemptuously refer to as literature: "La poésie est le contraire de la littérature. Elle règne sur les idoles de toute espèce et les illusions réalistes. ..." [87] In their eyes the efforts of the conventional prose writer and poet have been equally vain.

### The novel

From the first Manifesto, Surrealists set about attacking Realism and the tradition of the psychological novel. Realism, "hostile à tout essor intellectuel et moral."[88] André Breton published an appeal to bury Realism with Anatole France. Its sins were its insufficiency and its puerility. The style of information pure and simple betrays the petty aims of the Realists. Of what significance are the complacent ob-

[84] *Id., Histoire du Surréalisme*, p. 12.

[85] When Aragon returned from Russia he composed *Front rouge,* a revolutionary poem which aroused the French authorities. Breton rallied the Surrealists to Aragon's defense, maintaining that an artist's words do not engage him, that he should not be held responsible for his writings!

[86] "Seconde Arche," *Fontaine,* LXIII, 701–3.

[87] Breton and Eluard, "Notes sur la poésie," *La Révolution surréaliste,* XII, 53.

[88] Breton, "Premier Manifeste," *Les Manifestes du Surréalisme,* p. 17.

servations novelists feel compelled to record, their faithful and minute description of external trivia? Their descriptions have no more value than picture postcards. The real life of an individual is elsewhere, exposed only by an occasional chance gesture. Thus Breton signified his intention to relate the most outstanding episodes of his life only "telle que je peux la concevoir en dehors de son plan organique." [89] Why record the conventional patterns of existence when the significant events of the inner life escape them? Generally speaking, the novel is an inferior genre and Surrealism sees in its present popularity a sign of great decadence. The only novels susceptible of arousing Surrealist interest are those dominated by the *merveilleux* wherein the inner life is adequately represented: "Dans le domaine littéraire, le merveilleux seul est capable de féconder des oeuvres ressortissant à un genre inférieur tel que le roman et d'une façon générale tout ce qui participe de l'anecdote." [90] But there is no room for mystery in Realism. Everything is pre-arranged and the characters are completely solved. "L'intraitable manie qui consiste à ramener l'inconnu au connu, au classable, berce les cerveaux." [91] How far we are from the nineteenth-century French tradition stemming from Balzac, who stated in the *Avant-Propos* of *La Comédie humaine* his aspiration to be "l'archéologue du mobilier social, le nomenclateur des professions, l'enregistreur du bien et du mal ... !"

Especially anti-pathetical to the Surrealists is the tinkering with psychological data to which the Realists were addicted in the name of objectivity. Where Giraudoux mocked the patient novelist, working as if at a *jeu de patience,* Breton denounced with characteristic violence. In praise of Huysmans, he has this to say:

Comme je le sépare, est-il besoin de le dire, de tous les empiriques du roman qui prétendent mettre en scène des personnages distincts d'eux-mêmes et les campent physiquement, moralement, à leur manière, pour les besoins d'on préfère ne pas savoir quelle cause! D'un personnage réel, sur qui ils croient avoir quelques renseignements, ils font deux personnages de leur histoire; de deux, ils en font un. ... Eh bien, je ne trouve pas cela enfantin, je trouve cela monstrueux. Je persiste à réclamer les noms, à ne m'intéresser qu'aux livres qu'on laisse battants comme des portes, et desquels on n'a pas à chercher la clé.[92]

Happily, he concludes, the days of psychological literature "à affabulation romanesque" are about over. Only too long has the novel been cluttered by sterile discussions and psychological fabrications, has been used as a vessel of "médiocrité, de haine et de plate suffisance." [93]

### Poetry and the poet

The same artifice and petty objectives which have kept prose from dealing with the vital problems of man and his destiny beset poetry. Versification and studied arrangement have stifled the vital poetic impulse; care for form and search for

[89] *Id., Nadja,* p. 22.
[90] *Id.,* "Premier Manifeste," *Les Manifestes du Surréalisme,* p. 29.
[91] *Ibid.,* p. 21.
[92] Breton, *Nadja,* pp. 19–20.
[93] *Id.,* "Premier Manifeste," *Les Manifestes du Surréalisme,* p. 17.

beauty have led poets down a hopeless path. Tzara and the others observed that poetry not only could exist independently of the poem, but was actually obliged to. The eighteenth century offered abundant proof. At that time poetry seems to have fled from its metrical prison to take refuge in the effusions of Jean Jacques and in the scandalous confessions of Sade.

Such reflections upon the essential nature of poetry bore out the contention that language possesses an autonomy, a validity in itself. French poets had been more or less aware of this fact since Baudelaire, but Surrealists contended that many had failed to exploit the discovery properly by trying to master intellectually the mysterious force of word combinations. Thus they deplored the efforts of Mallarmé and his disciples, who labored to capture, according to Paul Valéry's expression, the "hydre poétique" in their studied constructions. Their error lay in conceiving of poetry as an exercise, not as an instinct. "Un poème doit être un débâcle de l'intellect. Il ne faut être autre chose." [94] On the other hand, all those who seemed to surrender completely were rewarded by the gift of poetic grace (Lautréamont, Rimbaud, etc.). Thus, the importance of the poet as a conscious factor in his poetry, which we have observed diminishing since German Romanticists abdicated in favor of inspiration and the trance, reached its minimum with Surrealism.

Real poetry is spontaneous—and fortuitous. Breton compares a work of art to a crystal. Like a crystal, it is a product of a spontaneous creation:

Qu'on entende bien que cette affirmation s'oppose pour moi, de la manière la plus catégorique, la plus constante, à tout ce qui tente, esthétiquement comme moralement, de fonder la beauté formelle sur un travail de perfectionnement volontaire auquel il appartiendrait à l'homme de se livrer. Je ne cesse pas, au contraire, d'être porté à l'apologie de la création, de l'action spontanée et cela dans la mesure même où le cristal, par définition non améliorable, en est l'expression parfaite.[95]

The creative artist has only to remain passive and let his unconscious self, that "hôte inconnu," dictate to him. Above all, he must not interfere. "A la moindre rature, le principe d'inspiration totale est ruiné. L'imbécilité efface ce que l'oreiller a prudemment créé." [96] Poetry has nothing to do with skill or talent. Surrealists proclaimed that they were devoid of talent: "Nous n'avons pas de talent ... nous qui nous sommes faits dans nos oeuvres ... les modestes *appareils enregistreurs.*" [97] André Breton gives the formula for Surrealist composition, a recipe of "une dérisoire simplicité":

Faites-vous apporter de quoi écrire, après vous être établi en un lieu aussi favorable que possible à la concentration de votre esprit sur lui-même. Placez-vous dans l'état le plus passif, ou réceptif que vous pourrez. Faites abstraction de votre génie, de vos talents et de ceux de tous les autres. Dites-vous bien que la littérature est un des plus tristes chemins qui mènent à tout. Ecrivez vite sans sujet préconçu, assez vite pour ne pas retenir et ne pas être tenté de vous relire. La première phrase viendra toute seule. ...[98]

[94] Breton and Eluard, "Notes sur la poésie," *La Révolution surréaliste*, XII, 53.
[95] Breton, *L'Amour fou*, p. 19.
[96] Breton and Eluard, "Notes sur la poésie," *La Révolution surréaliste*, XII, 54.
[97] Breton, "Premier Manifeste," *Les Manifestes du Surréalisme*, p. 48.
[98] *Ibid.*, p. 51.

The production is dependent entirely upon the caprice of the unconscious. Its quality differs in the same person according to moments and days, and of course according to individuals. In other words, according to the nature of inspiration. Inspiration, which found a large place in German esthetics, reappears in Surrealism as the dictate of the unconscious. "Le surréalisme est l'inspiration reconnue, acceptée et pratiquée." [99] There are some relevant differences however. It can no longer be thought of as a "chose sacrée," nor as an inexplicable visitation, but as a faculty in operation. Whereas former poets considered inspiration an infrequent mysterious visitor, the Surrealist's abandonment to the unconscious made him constantly receptive to inspiration. He is always a prophet, an "echo sonore," a seer.

Inspiration is invoked through the process of the "hasard objectif": certain unforeseen encounters, surprises, act as powerful stimuli. The apparently chance disposition of certain objects may awaken responses which the individual is at a loss to explain.

In an artist this feeling may unleash a great creative activity. Chirico could not paint, Breton affirms,[100] except when surprised by a certain disposition of objects. The whole enigma of revelation lay for him in the word surprise. Apollinaire, whose ideas contributed greatly to fecundate the Surrealist movement, had already noted the importance of surprise as a creative stimulus: "La surprise est le plus grand ressort nouveau. C'est par la surprise, par la place importante qu'il fait à la surprise, que l'esprit nouveau se distingue de tous les mouvements artistiques et littéraires qui l'ont précédé." [101] Breton adds: "La surprise doit être recherchée pour elle-même, inconditionnellement." [102] These intuitive flashes bypass the rational faculties entirely. Inspiration is instantaneous. It is recognizable by a feeling of being so totally possessed that no rational choice is possible. The individual feels acutely that he is the center of curious forces, that his inner self possesses an awareness and a complicity with forces which his intelligence cannot comprehend. Surrealism aimed to use every possible means of multiplying occasions for such short cuts.

Certain atmospheres proved more favorable to inspiration than others. Collaboration of two or more individuals was found more stimulating than independent effort. The muse who visited the Romantic poet only in the solitude of nature or his room preferred the company of Surrealists in groups. They have always conceived of poetry as being a collective enterprise. Herder's notion of the *Volkswerk* would receive their full approbation. One knows how many Surrealist works were undertaken jointly. Especially interesting are their parlor games: questions and answers, *qui pro quos* and *coq-à-l'âne* where impersonality and gratuity could be completely realized.

What distinguishes the poet from the rest of men? Surrealism denied him special gifts or talents; he is also without special favors in the matter of divination and

---

[99] Aragon, *Traité du Style,* p. 187.
[100] Breton, *Nadja,* p. 14.
[101] Apollinaire, "L'Esprit nouveau et les poètes," *Mercure de France,* December 1, 1918, p. 392.
[102] Breton, *L'Amour fou,* pp. 122–23.

oracle. Surrealists soon cured themselves of the temptation to see themselves in the rôle of prophets or diviners. Against the claim for special rank demanded for poets by the Germans and the French Symbolists, Surrealism maintains that the poet is only a man among men.[103] Poetry is not the privilege of a happy few. The statement of Lautréamont became a slogan: "La poésie doit être faite par tous, non par un." As Giraudoux had proclaimed, everyone is an "élu."

With Surrealism we have seen the revolt against the intellectual and the conventional pushed to its final conclusions. What the Germans recommended, but more times than not, did not themselves practice, is completely carried out. Their theory has become a fact. Surrealists recognized their movement as the most recent development in the Romantic cycle which Hegel defined in his *Esthetics*. Freed of traditional problems of verbal expression and formal perfection, the process has amounted to a gradual despoiling of all the customary attributes of literature. Nothing remains but curiously evocative rhythms and fortuitous images, hinting at man's fundamental nature. Everything precise, particular, personal, indicative, elaborated is banished. Poetry is reduced to a basic gesture. Literature is replaced by incantation and magic situated at the dawn of consciousness. What Jean Cassou says of "L'Homme approximatif" of Tristan Tzara may be taken to describe the Surrealist achievements: "Ici ... aucune des ressources où la poésie a ordinairement puisé ses charmes de suggestion. Seul, le désordre, l'ingénieux, le hasardeux désordre, a présidé à cet événement. ... On touche ici aux sources mêmes de la vie poétique, à ces centres nerveux." [104]

A word of caution. Is a poem the same thing as the dream? Surrealists hesitated before this affirmation which might seem the logical conclusion of their theory. The participation of the intellect cannot be dispensed with entirely. Not that the dream is not esthetic in itself, but because the virtue of the poem transcends the purely esthetic, it demands the collaboration of both the conscious and unconscious faculties. One will remember Breton rebuked poets who, content with the esthetic achievements of automatic texts, did not submit their production to an intellectual scrutiny. Paul Eluard makes a clean distinction between an automatic text and a poem, and defines poetic unity as an equilibrium of internal and external elements. Here, too, the poet's concern is metaphysical more than esthetic:

On ne prend pas le récit d'un rêve pour un poème. Tous deux réalité vivante, mais le premier est souvenir, tout de suite usé, transformé, une aventure, et du deuxième rien ne se perd, ne se change. Le poème désensibilise l'univers au seul profit des facultés humaines, permet à l'homme de voir autrement, d'autres choses. Son ancienne vision est morte, ou fausse. Il découvre un nouveau monde, il devient un nouvel homme.

On a pu penser que l'écriture automatique rendait les poèmes inutiles. Non: elle

---

[103] There has been some uncertainty regarding the attitude of the Surrealists in this matter. Breton, in his second Manifesto, did call for the "occultation profonde, véritable du surréalisme." (*Les Manifestes du Surréalisme*, p. 169.) But his motive seems to be his fear of succumbing to popular success and creating a "poncif." It is the approbation of the public, not the principle of collective creative effort that he seems to oppose.

[104] *Pour la poésie*, p. 265.

augmente, développe seulement le champ de l'examen de conscience poétique, en l'enrichissant. Si la conscience est parfaite, les éléments que l'écriture automatique extrait du monde intérieur et les éléments du monde extérieur s'équilibrent. Réduits alors à égalité, ils s'entremêlent, se confondent pour former l'unité poétique.[105]

## Conclusion

In casting a comprehensive glance over the entire Surrealist production, one is compelled to conclude that, like German Romanticism, the school is rich in theory but poor in works. Paradoxically, these two schools which based their esthetic upon opposition to the rational, should owe their fame to their expositions and analyses of the poetic art. We could say of Surrealism what the venerable Brandes wrote of German Romanticism: "Seldom has any poetic school worked under such a weight of perpetual consciousness of its own character as did this." [106] The dearth of creative monuments which calls forth the suspicions of some commentators is only partly due to their failure to realize their convictions. It is largely the inevitable result of their fundamental ideas. The work of art is not considered an end in itself, but as a means to an end. Liberation, not communication, is its incentive. There is no point in its survival as soon as its mission is accomplished. It is therefore inconceivable that Surrealism should have produced an important body of work to be conserved by posterity. Such would be contrary to its fundamental aim. The major contribution of Surrealism, like that of German Romanticism, lies in the orientation it offers subsequent writers. Both probed deeply into the sources of the poetic imagination. Their elucidations and affirmations have kept poets mindful of true poetic values. Their explorations into the subconscious and the metaphysical have opened fields which new writers are cultivating with enthusiasm.

[105] Eluard, *Donner à voir*, p. 147.
[106] Brandes, *op. cit.*, pp. 41–42.

# CHAPTER THREE

# A General View

L'histoire littéraire trouve les plus troublantes analogies entre les tendances maîtresses de la "nouvelle" littérature française et les dominantes du Romantisme allemand d'avant Jéna.[1]

THE DOCTRINES and practices which we have observed that Jean Giraudoux and the Surrealists share with the German Romantics are fundamental in twentieth-century literature. These characteristics cannot be mistaken by anyone gazing over the panorama of the last fifty years, whether his intention be to praise or indict, or merely to label. All the great names of the period—Gide, Valéry, Claudel, Alain-Fournier, Proust—and many minor ones offer further illustration of what we have studied in Giraudoux and Breton.

## THE HISTORICAL LINK WITH GERMAN ROMANTICISM

### Philosophy

Although our concern is to survey affinities and not to determine influences, except when writers cut back directly to German sources, we should not give the impression that similarities are a fortuitous encounter. It is, for example, particularly significant that German thought had acquired a place of increasing importance in the French educational system during the years following the Franco-Prussian War. In 1902 Pierre Lasserre deplored that the situation was "tout à la mode germanique."[2] Although Fichte and Schelling did not create a school in France by their metaphysics, their transcendental implications regarding humanity, history, religion and art found fertile terrain. "Ces vues, ces rêves, sont les principaux éléments de cette grande fermentation endémique de l'esprit germanique dans la pensée française."[3] German language and philosophy were administered in heavy doses to modern writers from their lycée days. Mme Renée Lang, speaking of Gide, notes that the metaphysics he absorbed in his youth was taught in the majority of French secondary schools in the last two decades of the nineteenth century. The young men took a passionate interest in German philosophy, for it offered an escape from the grim positivism of their elders and a consolation in their confused world. "La doctrine de Fichte mettait en déroute l'intellectualisme au profit d'une faculté 'supra-sensible et supra-rationnelle' qui libérait délicieusement l'âme des jeunes poètes des entraves quotidiennes et que Bergson n'allait pas tarder

---

[1] Fernand Baldensperger, *La Littérature française entre les deux guerres, 1919–1939* (Los Angeles: Lymanhouse, 1941), p. 175.

[2] "Enquête sur l'influence allemande," *Mercure de France*, XLIV (1902), 340.

[3] Pierre Lasserre, *Le Romantisme français* (Calmann-Lévy, 1919), p. 472.

à convertir en 'intuition'." [4] They could say with young Gide, "Ah, la philosophie allemande trouvait en moi un terrain bien propice." [5]

Gide is quite frank about his debt to Fichte. He states: "Schopenhauer et Fichte m'ont nourri, m'ont formé, ont décidé de ma pensée à un âge où celle-ci voit se dresser devant elle les grands problèmes." [6] His interest in Fichte persisted long. In 1894 he noted in his journal: "Durant deux automnes aussi j'ai lu Fichte; cette année vais-je avoir le temps? J'ai pris avec moi, par provision, *la Doctrine de la Science*." [7] Gide's early works, the *Cahiers, Traités, Voyages* seem to stem directly from German philosophy. Mme Lang calls the *Traité du Narcisse* a perfect illustration of the Fichtean doctrine.

The influence of philosophers associated with German Romanticism was re-inforced by that of contemporary French thinkers who are in many ways their heirs. In philosophy proper, the main currents of French thought in the twentieth century show an interesting affinity to the early nineteenth-century German. Bergson in particular joins the champions of subjectivism, liberty and the foes of rationalism and empiricism across the Rhine. His contact with the German Romantics has been studied by Dr. Carl Dyrssen of Marburg, who points out the influence of Ravaisson, Bergson's teacher and a disciple of German idealism. Bergson, according to Professor Dyrssen, is the heir of Fichte, Schelling, and Novalis. Typical of Dyrssen's interesting linkings is the tracing of Bergson's *élan vital* back through the *effort* of Maine de Biran, to Bouterweks' *lebendiger Kraft der Individualität*, hence to the *Ich-Begriff* of Fichte. Bergson agrees with Schelling in his notion of art: "Beide glauben sie, in der künstlerischen Production das Leben selbst in seiner ganzen Unmittelbarkeit zu fassen, zu erfahren." [8] However, the French and German philosophers differ on other points. Bergson's emphasis upon action does not harmonize with Schelling's reluctance to descend from the level of theory and speculation. Bergson believed that speculation is a luxury, whereas action is a necessity, and that we think only to act. To reconcile the two points of view Dyrssen introduces Novalis. Novalis is the great unifier. His efforts were constantly directed toward reconciling the apparently dissimilar and antithetical. He maintained that thought is only action transformed: "Das Denken ist wie die Blüte gewiß nichts als die feinste Evolution der plastischen Kräfte—und nur die allgemeine Naturkraft in der n—Dignität." [9] Bergson was always quite reticent as to his sources, but Dyrssen believes that he was a conscious disciple of the Romantic philosophers with Novalis functioning as go-between and reconciler.

---

[4] Renée Lang, *André Gide et la pensée allemand* (Egloff, 1949), p. 17.

[5] *Journal 1889–1939* (Ed. de la Pléiade, 1939), p. 800.

[6] *Oeuvres complètes* (Gallimard, 1932–39), XV, 513.

[7] *Journal*, p. 51. This is the work which had taught Friedrich Schlegel also that the world of sense perception is to be surpassed, that the only thing which has real existence is the active ego which realizes itself in the everlasting becoming.

[8] Carl Dyrssen, *Bergson und die deutsche Romantik* (Marburg: Braun, 1922), p. 24.

[9] Novalis, *Schriften*, III, 272.

Existentialism, which succeeds Bergsonism as the most noteworthy philosophic movement in twentieth-century France, is patently an outgrowth of Germanic thought. Kierkegaard was not only sympathetic with the German Romantic point of view but directly influenced by its philosophic and literary theories.[10] Jaspers and Heidegger transmitted the Danish philosopher's thought to Sartre and others who have adapted it into a French philosophy which stands as the most recent protest against rational and positivistic tradition. Sartre, like so many French philosophers since early nineteenth century, had a year of study in Germany. Through Husserl's lectures he came in direct contact with the Germanic current. It is not my purpose here to undertake any exposé of the school of Sartre even though no philosophy has been more intimately tied up with literature. I should, however, try to indicate briefly how close the fundamental assumptions of Existentialism are to those of German Romanticism and those already suggested by philosophers and writers of the early 1900's.

As its name indicates, Existentialism emphasizes existence and the concrete instead of essences, the abstract and the mathematical. Subjectivism is the point of departure. Kierkegaard stated that subjectivity is truth. Everyone has the choice of creating his own world. That is to say, individual liberty is assured by the power man has of giving his own meaning and interpretation to things and events which concern him. Thus the individual can assert his will even in a universe otherwise deterministic. The Existentialist has a profound sense of the irrationality of reality. He admits no norm nor the fundamental validity of rational standards. Kierkegaard said that everything he saw, he saw in contradiction, that life was nothing but contradiction.[11] What appears in Existentialism to conflict with the attitude maintained by both German and contemporary French Romanticism is the denial of ideality. Whereas Fichte affirmed the transcendental nature of the ego and proceeded from there toward metaphysical speculation, Kierkegaard and his line remain in the concrete. Existentialism is as suspicious of metaphysics as of logic. The faith in the absolute seems either utterly lacking among Existentialists or else turned into religious faith, as with the Christian Existentialists. The Atheists remaining in the philosophy of the absurd seem to have taken the choice of the fantasists and ironists.

Philip Blair Rice, reviewing the trends of contemporary French philosophy, has this to say: "All the philosophical schools are deeply tinged with that *Idéalisme* or *Spiritualisme* which has long been the dominant influence in the universities, and which in turn has undergone periodic influences from German Idealism, gallicizing it in importing it across the Rhine." [12] In the case of Existentialism, which flatly rejects any ideal world, the gallicization process seems to be considerably more than a slight modification. Hegel and Sartre seem fundamentally opposed.

The interest in German philosophy and its contribution to the new French philosophy has done much to push twentieth-century literature into the path of the

---

[10] It is interesting to note that he turned from Hegel back to Schelling.

[11] *Journal* (Extracts), Gallimard, 1941, p. 210.

[12] Philip Blair Rice, "Children of Narcissus," *Kenyon Review*, XII (1950), 122.

German Romantics. German philosophy has been so much "in the air" that French writers who seem to owe so much to a German may be totally unacquainted with his works. A knowledge of the writer may come later, after philosophy has prepared the way for a sympathetic understanding.[13] This seems to be the case with André Gide and German authors. Mme Lang points out the many points of similarity between the *Cahiers d'André Walter* and Novalis. The latter's maxim "Life is a soul sickness" could be written across the entire work. In both one finds the same mingling of dream and reality, etc. But she doubts if Gide knew Novalis at the time of writing. As in the case of Nietzsche, the actual encounter postdates what appears to be nothing short of modeling.

But writers like Gide were not long in discovering their kindred spirits across the Rhine. Maeterlinck had found Novalis first and it is he who introduced him to Gide. They resolved to undertake a translation together: Maeterlinck published the *Fragmente* and *Die Lehrlinge zu Sais,* but Gide never carried out his project for *Heinrich von Ofterdingen.* His enthusiasm at the time, however, is unmistakable: "Il faudra traduire *Heinrich von Ofterdingen* sans plus attendre. J'ai songé aussi à *Peter Schlemihl* qu'on connait si peu; et *Ondine* de la Motte." [14] In the *Voyage d'Urien* we can see the direct influence of Novalis. It owes much to the *Lehrlinge zu Sais,* even to the inclusion of a whole passage from the model. All during this period Gide was deeply imbued with the style of the German Romantic authors. He is still reading them at the time of his trip to Algeria with his wife: "Puis nous prîmes, sitôt à Biskra, *Der Geheimnisvolle* de Tieck. . . ." [15] Jean Paul, Hoffmann, Kleist, Eichendorff, Hölderlin kept Gide for long in direct contact with the German Romantic spirit.

*Symbolism*

An historical link between contemporary French writing and German Romanticism even greater than philosophy may be found in literature proper. This is of course the Symbolist school. Romantic ideas reached modern writers in their enormous inheritance from Symbolism which they have never ceased to exploit. The German influence in French Symbolism is investigated in Reynaud's monumental but very partisan study, *L'Influence allemande en France au XVIII et au XIX siècle.* He establishes Wagner, who realized more fully than anyone else in Germany the ideals and doctrines of the Romantic School, as the source of French Symbolism: "C'est de toutes ces influences germaniques ou septentrionales réunies, mais surtout celle de Wagner, que naquit chez nous l'école 'symboliste'. . . ." [16] According to Guy Michaud's genealogical chart, German Romanticism passes

---

[13] This would seem to be Edmond Jaloux's meaning when he speaks of a project to translate the German Romantic authors: "Cela permettra à beaucoup de lettrés de prendre connaissance d'une littérature qui a joué un grand rôle dans l'histoire des idées du XIXe siècle et qui est à peu près inconnue en France." (*Du Rêve à la réalité,* p. 82.)

[14] *Journal,* p. 39.

[15] *Ibid.,* p. 146.

[16] Louis Reynaud, *L'Influence allemande en France au XVIII et au XIX siècle* (Hachette, 1922), p. 279.

through Wagner and Carlyle [17] to Baudelaire, who is the direct source of Symbolist esthetics.[18] Wagner's prestige and popularity in France disseminated German Romantic notions widely. The tenets of the new school are identical with those already enunciated by Novalis and Schlegel.[19] The "symbol" itself can be cited. The Symbolist aim to suggest the intimate correspondences which they discovered between man and nature, between the intelligible and the unintelligible, does not differ from the quest of Novalis. Schelling's philosophy underlies both:

Das Kunstwerk reflektiert uns die Identität der bewußten und der bewußtlosen Tätigkeit.

Das *An-sich* der Poesie ist nun das aller Kunst: es ist Darstellung des Absoluten oder des Universum in einem Besonderen.[20]

What the *Revue Wagnerienne* and the *Revue indépendante* called Wagnerian literature and philosophy was nothing other than the idealism of Fichte and Schelling.

Both schools strove to exploit the musicality of language to express the unexpressable, the dimly perceived. Mallarmé dreamed of making the poem a simple combination of sonorities, similar to the Wagnerian symphony.

Les symbolistes français et les romantiques allemands se sont persuadés que les lois constitutives de l'art du vers sont des lois musicales de rythme et d'harmonie, et qu'il convient de demander au vers non plus un rythme trop souvent factice, mais un rythme basé réellement sur les sensations auditives produites par la lecture normale du vers. Ils désirèrent des combinaisons harmoniques plus fines, plus discrètes, plus immatérielles, ce qui fut la cause des réformes de langage: extension du vocabulaire usuel, emploi de mots archaïques et de néologismes.[21]

Besides Wagner, Schopenhauer and Nietzsche must be cited as additional vehicles to transmit German Romanticism into France. They offered Symbolists strength in their campaign against positivism and modern social existence. Nietzsche could tell them that man was not the slave of determinism but a free individual. Schopenhauer demonstrated that the exterior world is illusion. Thus through Symbolism the fundamentals of Romanticism such as subjectivity, individualism, liberty, idealism are reaffirmed and firmly established as the "myths" of modern literature.

[17] It is interesting to note that John Charpentier reduces most of the influence of German thought upon Symbolism to indirect filtering through English writers. (*De Joseph Delorme à Paul Claudel,* Les Oeuvres Représentatives, 1931.)

[18] Guy Michaud, *Message poétique du Symbolisme* (Nizet, 1947), appendix I.

[19] There is the same reaction against Naturalism; the same esthetic basis: idealism and intuition; the same desire to express the unexpressable; the same research and reforms in prosody; the same love of folklore and popular songs; the same propensity toward irony and religiousness. (See Tancrède de Visan, *L'Attitude du lyrisme contemporain,* Mercure de France, 1911, p. 397.)

[20] Schelling, "System des transzendentalen Idealismus," *Deutsche Literatur,* ser. 17, vol. III, p. 245.

———, "Philosophie der Kunst," *ibid.,* p. 256.

[21] Jean Thorel, "Les Romantiques allemands et les Symbolistes français," *Entretiens politiques et littéraires,* September, 1891. (Text reproduced in G. Michaud, *La Doctrine symboliste, Documents,* Nizet, 1947, p. 90.)

Contemporary Romanticism harks back to the German school through philosophy and the French Symbolistic school, which is after all only a succedaneum.[22]

Ramenée en France au lendemain de la guerre par Kant et Schopenhauer, qu'accompagnaient les fameuses «méthodes germaniques», puis par Wagner, par Nietzsche, par le marxisme, l'influence allemande semblait, vers le début du XXe siècle, plus solide et plus puissante que jamais chez nous.[23]

Tancrède de Visan sees contemporary literature as an outgrowth of a vast ideological and historical movement. Symbolism (which includes twentieth-century poets) he defines as lyrical manifestations of philosophic idealism.[24] Among the great masters of contemporary literature, probably none has drawn his inspiration as directly as Giraudoux from German Romantic sources. Yet indirect as their contacts may have been, modern French writers have arrived at a position in regard to literature and life which coincides with the theories of Novalis and the Schlegels.

There remains to mention contemporary events as a significant factor in turning writers in the direction of German Romanticism. The disillusioned postwar generations were readily disposed to abandon French traditional values and customs. The catastrophe of war seemed proof enough that intelligence does not rule or even explain the world. Moreover, modern man has become increasingly irritated by social routine and a life built upon an eight-hour day. He has longed to escape from the futile and pretentious world inherited from the partisans of reason and science. Escape and repudiation ring all through French literature.

### The Widespread Adherence to the Romantic Creed

Julien Benda, leader of the opposition and staunch defender of the French rationalistic tradition, analyzes quite accurately, in spite of his hostility, the dominant tenets of contemporary Romanticism. He admits as basic the desire to break with the aims and rules of intellectualism and declares the mystic viewpoint to pertain today in all esthetic matters. In Benda's discussion of the various implications of the modern trend we can observe how widespread those attitudes are which we surveyed in Giraudoux, Breton, and the Germans.

*Attitude toward man and the universe*

Twentieth-century French writers have accepted generally the Romantic dogma of subjectivism, and defended its major derivatives of liberty, individualism, particularity. The subjective is the undisputed criterion of all values, and objective reality has become a meaningless phrase. Gide, Proust, Valéry admit only solipsistic knowledge. We have already studied the Germanic origins of this attitude. Julien Benda cites Kierkegaard as anticipating the modern French writers. He is reminded of Proust when he hears the founder of Existentialism say, "To exist means first of all to be an individual"; of Valéry, when Kierkegaard says, "From the esthetic and

---

[22] René de Gourmont, "L'Idéalisme," *Le Chemin de velours* (Paris, 1902), p. 221.
[23] Reynaud, *op. cit.,* p. 287.
[24] Tancrède de Visan, *op. cit.,* p. 7.

intellectual point of view, to investigate reality is an error"; and of Gide, when he hears, "From the ethical point of view, to investigate the reality of another person is an error, for one can investigate only one's own." [25] Kierkegaard speaks for them all when he says that subjectivity is truth, subjectivity is reality. Sartre is a faithful disciple of the master. For him man is the creator and animator of the universe. Other prominent apostles of subjectivity are identified by Marcel Raymond. Poets such as Léon-Paul Fargue, Milosz, Alain-Fournier, he says, seem to live in a purely subjective world. They have recreated the *patrie intérieure* of the German poets where one finds the same dreams, fables, legends, the marvelous of the *Märchen*. Subjectivity in the field of ideas, individualism in the field of action. The case of Gide is perhaps the most outstanding, but the fantasists and the humorists—all the eccentrics and *affranchis*—also contributed to the insurrection of the individual.

Of the postwar writers, a recent critic can say, "Un Camus, un Bernanos, un Anouilh, un Sartre, un Aragon, un Malraux ... il est en eux quelque chose de commun, c'est que chacun de leurs héros a pour aventure de construire son destin dans la solitude, sans le secours d'une norme sociale ou d'une grâce divine. ..." [26]

The modern insistence is wholly upon the particular. "Aujourd'hui, où la pensée ne prétend plus à l'universel ..." says Camus.[27] If Proust discovers the universal in his characters, it is by studying them in their individuality.[28] The universal is reached only by an extension of the individual. The classicists and realists conceived of personalities *sub specie aeterni*. Balzac, in the *Avant Propos à la Comédie humaine* sets down as the business of the writer to be "un peintre plus ou moins fidèle, plus ou moins heureux, patient ou courageux des types humains." Although professional varieties exist, like biological varieties, "il n'y a qu'un animal!" But since Bergson, writers have eschewed intellectual generalities: "La verité est que dans chaque cas l'attention est marquée d'une nuance spéciale et comme individualisée par l'objet auquel elle s'applique." [29] Valéry says, "Il n'y a d'universel que ce qui est suffisamment grossier pour l'être." [30]

Intuition replaces intellectual analysis as a means of understanding. "L'idéalisme allemand nous a malgré tout influencés ... et nous avons délaissé l'imagination romantique pour l'intuition des Ravaisson et des Bergson." [31] The message which Bergson preached was echoed through Cubism, through Proust and all his school.

---

[25] Julien Benda, *La France Byzantine* (Gallimard, 1945), p. 81. Note Gide: "C'est en nous qu'est la réalité; notre esprit crée ses propres vérités." *Oeuvres complètes*, I, 54.

[26] R. M. Albérès, *La Révolte des écrivains d'aujourd'hui* (Corrêa, 1949), p. 15.

[27] *Le Mythe de Sisyphe* (Gallimard, 1942), p. 137.

[28] "La grande découverte du psychologisme—à laquelle Proust a le plus contribué en France,— c'est que l'art n'avait jamais étudié l'«individu», mais s'était toujours contenté d'incarner des «notions», plus ou moins riches d'humanité. L'effort et le tourment de la littérature d'aujourd'hui, ont été précisément de traduire l'unicité de l'individu, au lieu de s'arrêter au nominalisme de la psychologie courante." (Benjamin Crémieux, *Inventaires 1918–1930,* Corrêa, 1931), p. 88.

[29] Bergson, *Les Deux Sources de la morale et de la religion* (Geneva: Skira, 1945), p. 46.

[30] Valéry, *Mauvaises Pensées* (Gallimard, 1942), p. 174.

[31] Tancrède de Visan, *op. cit.,* p. 314.

They proceed, not by studying something from the outside, but by an act of mystic communion where the subject fuses with the object.

Knowledge comes as a sudden insight into the nature of the object. It is not acquired slowly or methodically, or even consciously. "Car c'est à l'endroit où l'homme semble sur le point de finir que probablement il commence." This sentence which was suggested to Maurice Maeterlinck through his study of Novalis could, according to Tancrède de Visan,[32] be set in burning letters on the banner of contemporary poetry. Modern writers show Fichte to be wrong when he stated that only Germans were capable of spontaneous intuition. Spontaneity has replaced development and integration in the thought process.

Hence the utterances of the Romantics take characteristically the form of gratuitous affirmations. Gide, Valéry, Suarès, Alain-Fournier, Péguy are all given to remarks of ideological pretension unsustained by logical justification, proof, reference, even discussion. It is what Benda calls ideological lyricism, and he offers an example from Les Nourritures terrestres: "Que l'homme est né pour le bonheur, certes toutes la nature l'enseigne." He quotes Suarès from Debussy: "Il en est là comme en science: on donne le nom suprême de simplicité à la banalité et à l'ignorance."[33] Valéry is particularly given to phrases of an oracular quality: "Mais malheureuse même, et même moribonde, une société ne peut pas se regarder sans rire."[34] What we have here are ideas treated as lyric themes. Views upon politics, art, history, science are expressed as personally, as subjectively as we are accustomed to deal with sentiments. Alain-Fournier, for example, can discuss Plato, Kant, Auguste Comte, in a purely lyrical manner without invoking a single text.

The characteristic expression of the period is the poetic hypothesis, the random assertion. Like the Germans, modern French poets would be philosophers. "Die Trennung von Poet und Denker ist nur scheinbar. . . ."[35] Their approach to intellectual problems is affective, that is to say, esthetic. Carefully weighed, systematically proposed ideas give way before striking and paradoxical assertions. They subscribe to Schlegel's belief that "Paradox ist alles, was groß und gut ist." The spontaneity and arbitrariness of their thoughts lead them to the fragmentary style which was so popular with the Germans. It is further evidence of the prevalent disdain for form and system. It should be noted in this connection that the short pithy utterances of the contemporary writer and of the German Romantic are quite different from the maxims of a La Rochefoucauld or a Chamfort. Supporting the traditional French maxim is a system, of which the maxim is a concentrated expression. It implies the possibility of demonstration and proof. The German phrases are in effect fragments, arbitrary and whimsical, whose validity is wholly personal. For the most part they are collections of impressions, noted in their spontaneity. Discontinuity has replaced sustained reasoning and a logical sequence of ideas. Valéry

---

[32] Ibid.
[33] Benda, op. cit., p. 89.
[34] Valéry, Variété II (Gallimard, 1929), p. 66.
[35] Novalis (see Chapter I, note 16).

compares the new way with the old "Il (Bossuet) procède par constructions, tandis que nous procédons par accidents." [36]

Since all systems are to be avoided, the modern thinker is inclined, rather than to think out carefully and clearly his ideas, to offer them in the imprecise, untested state in which they occur to him. The clear idea with sharply defined contours is viewed with grave suspicion. Mallarmé and the Symbolists had attacked the validity of the clear idea: "La logique usuelle figurait à Mallarmé la banalité, le prévu, le fait d'être pensé au lieu de penser. Dans l'élan droit d'un raisonnement, d'un argument, il flairait le prestige, l'erreur, la grossièrté oratoires. Il sentait que l'on ne peut avoir raison que par intuitions brèves, que la raison de l'une de ces intuitions ne se continue pas dans sa voisine." [37] His descendants have never abandoned the fight. In the early part of our century when Symbolism seemed dead, little groups and reviews such as the *Ermitage, La Phalange, Occident, Vers et Prose,* etc., sprang up sporadically to reaffirm the anti-rationalist credo. Typical of the neo-symbolists is Jean Royère who celebrated the cult of Mallarmé by declaring that he was not over-much concerned by French clarity, that his poetry was obscure like the lily! Maeterlinck said that we live by hidden truths, what we know is not interesting. The very great among the writers of the twentieth century, zealous sons of Symbolism, have carried on the struggle, attacking the clear idea not only in poetry but in all fields of literature and art. Proust, Gide, Valéry, Claudel would unreservedly endorse Novalis' remark that a too clear vision of things sacrifices the sentiment of the indistinct, the magic intuition of things. Even such distant fields as those of science seem to be affected today.

It is chiefly the static quality attributed to the clearly defined idea which makes it inacceptable to writers of today. Julien Benda declares they will have nothing fixed, nothing stable. Everything fixed is dead. Every arrested idea is defunct. These are characteristic of the maxims Benda collects from modern writers.[38] Gide rephrases Valéry's thought: "Les idées nettes sont les plus dangereuses parce qu'alors on n'ose plus en changer et c'est anticipation de la mort." [39] Their position is no different from Fichte's from which the Germans conducted their anti-rationalist campaign. For Fichte it is the imprecise character of representations which indicates their most profound truth. Lasserre, incensed by the views expressed in the *Reden an die deutsche Nation,* burst forth indignantly:

Ce paysan fanatique est incapable de voir dans les disciplines, les instruments, les seuls instruments possibles, des conquêtes intellectuelles et des créations humaines en général; et la plus haute puissance de l'esprit lui apparaît sous les espèces de je ne sais quel laisser-aller infini qui ne peut engendrer que la tautologie, le rien mental. ... Il voit dans la Définition la mort de la pensée.[40]

[36] Valéry, *Variété II,* p. 44.
[37] Albert Thibaudet, *La Poésie de Stéphane Mallarmé* (Gallimard, 1926), p. 131.
[38] Benda, *op. cit.,* p. 18.
[39] Gide, *Prétextes* (Mercure de France, 1903), p. 125.
[40] *Op. cit.,* p. 483.

The violence of Lasserre's incriminations is of no avail against the modern writers who apparently are irremediably "germanized." "Das immer Werdende" is a principle which dominates the whole modern viewpoint. Thought must be fluid and constantly moving. It may not adopt any fixed position whatsoever. Valéry says of his Monsieur Teste: "Cet homme avait connu de bonne heure l'importance de ce qu'on pourrait nommer la *plasticité* humaine. ... Combien il avait dû rêver à sa propre malléabilité." [41]

Modern insistence upon the "fluid concept" is illustrated by the prevalent notion of personality. Personality does not appear in contemporary literature as static or single, but as fluid and multiple as in the *Märchen*. Precise identity dissolves in the countless diversity of its aspects. Bergson identified the ego with "duration"; modern writers are bent on capturing certain of its elusive and constantly changing aspects. The work of Proust in particular is an account of his heterogeneous identities. He muses on the "moi" which he was when he had his hair cut, the "moi" who sat for the first time in an armchair while Albertine was away, etc. The hero of a modern novel undergoes constant metamorphoses in his personality. His career, as exemplified by Giraudoux's protagonists, is often the vain search for an elusive identity.[42] Benjamin Crémieux makes the following observation: "A la faillite du monde extérieur s'est ajouté la faillite du monde intérieur, du moins d'un monde intérieur stable et donné une fois pour toutes. La période 1918-1930 restera dans l'histoire littéraire celle de la dissociation de la personnalité." [43]

The ego, freed from the confines which intellectualism has placed around it, can soar to the greatest heights. Nothing is to prevent its complete absorption into the universe. The mystic ecstasy of the German Romantic soul is the goal of the twentieth-century writer who aspires to surpass the limits conventionally imposed upon the individual to communicate with the absolute. Bergson had reaffirmed that the individual, upon uncovering his profound ego, reaches the essence of the world. So Jean Florence could write in *Phalange* (1912): "Si Bergson est un précurseur, c'est pour avoir reconnu l'absolu dans le subjectif." And Tancrède de Visan, speaking of Maeterlinck, could note: "Bientôt l'homme se rend compte que ce moi doit être de même essence que le moi universel et que le principe qui préside à l'organisation cosmique ... Dieu veut des dieux, dirait Fichte." [44] In a state akin to ecstasy, the poet enters into communion with the whole cosmos. "Je suis ivre d'avoir bu tout l'univers," says Guillaume Apollinaire.[45]

The three myths of modern writers, according to Albert Béguin, are the soul, the unconscious, poetry. Although reason may divide our being into faculties, make of it a machine which can be taken apart, there remains a longing to find integration, a fervent conviction that our being has a living essence which escapes analysis,

[41] *Monsieur Teste* (Gallimard, 1929), pp. 29–30.
[42] See also such works as Philippe Soupault, *Le Bon Apôtre*.
[43] Crémieux, *op. cit.*, p. 74.
[44] Tancrède de Visan, *op. cit.*, p. 103.
[45] Apollinaire, "Vendimiaire," *Alcools* (Gallimard, 1932), p. 169.

that is to say, a soul. The soul transcends the limits of waking existence, inhabits the states of ecstasy and the dream. Here are regions which the contemporary poet, after the German Romantic, will explore: "La descente aux profondeurs de l'être, la confiance accordée aux révélations du songe, de la folie, des vertiges et des extases, l'esprit du poète aux écoutes des dons du hasard, telles sont les démarches qui apparentent les romantiques allemands à nos poètes actuels." [46] Jacques Rivière offers to lead the way, "J'allumerai la lampe des songes; je descendrai dans l'abîme." He invites his contemporaries to behold the "vertigineuse réalité des premiers âges" in "le grand tournoiement silencieux des rêves." [47] The inspiration of the dream is of primary importance to all forms of contemporary writing. Its material—products of the unconscious mind—is endowed with extraordinary significance and is deemed the proper material of art; its method, the uncontrolled flow of images, is the technique of "automatic writing" which has been granted particular values in our times.

In contrast to the static nature of the intellectual process, the dream is perfectly mobile. The fixed hierarchy of values which forms the basis for social relations and rational thought is repudiated in the dream. The image replaces the rational concept; the metaphor replaces the syllogism. Motivation in the dream is whimsical and personal. All states of consciousness can possess equal significance. Trivial things are elevated and what is conventionally considered important reduced in a process of constant movement. Nothing remains isolated for long, but blends with everything else.

The dream suggests a deeper and truer reality than that of daily existence, a life apart from contingencies and a place of communication with the cosmic. For here the power of time and space is broken. One lives in a perpetual present, that is to say in eternity. This, we remember, was Novalis' firm conviction. Man can thus hope to glimpse and enjoy the divine in this world. "Le monde supérieur est plus proche de nous que nous ne le pensons ordinairement. *Ici-bas déjà,* nous vivons en lui et nous l'apercevons, étroitement mêlé à la trame de la nature terrestre." André Rousseaux links all the great modern dreamers—Proust, Alain-Fournier, Gide— with Novalis.[48] For them the words of Ofterdingen become prophetic: "Die Welt wird Traum; der Traum wird Welt."

The data of the unconscious are valued as superior knowledge, as revelation. The myth of poetry—its association with the unrational and its metaphysical claims— has been analyzed in connection with Giraudoux and the Surrealists. We may add to these two examples. Poetry has become again the vehicle for all secular mystic strivings: "Chez toute une école de poètes actuels, qui pourraient prendre pour devise: Par la poésie vers l'extase au sens originel du mot (exstare)." "La mission de la poésie est de permettre au moi d'échapper à ses limites et de se dilater

---

[46] Béguin, "Les Romantiques allemands et l'inconscient," *Le Romantisme allemand,* p. 94.

[47] Jacques Rivière, *Introduction à la Métaphysique du rêve.* (Cited by Raymond, *op. cit.,* p. 220.)

[48] André Rousseaux, *Littérature du XXᵉ siècle* (Albin Michel, 1938), I, 217.

jusqu'à l'infini." [49] "Le poète pénètre dans le primordial, il est le déchiffreur." [50] With Claudel: "... vision esthétique et vision mystique s'identifient ... il importe que le poète écarte l'épais tissu des habitudes et des conventions ancestrales pour saisir le réel dans sa nudité." [51] Apollinaire says, "Vous trouverez trace de prophétie dans la plupart des ouvrages conçus d'après l'esprit nouveau." [52] Jules Romains, no great friend of Symbolism, remains, nonetheless, in the Romantic tradition by his notion of the poet's mission: "Nous ne pensions pas que le poète dût aller moins loin que le philosophe dans le secret des choses." [53] Luc Durtain and the rest of his group also conceive of the poetic sense as an instrument of metaphysical exploration and conquest. Tancrède de Visan, in his studies on the *Attitude du lyrisme contemporain,* defines as the sole legitimate aim of poetry the attempt to express the ineffable, to attain a knowledge of hidden realities. French literary historians do not hesitate to link this widespread contemporary notion of the prestige of poetry with the German tradition: "Cette poétique ... s'appuie sur des intuitions et des croyances métaphysiques, qui sont celles-là même du romantisme allemand." [54] Benda singles out Proust, but implies the same for the rest of the "Byzantines":

L'oeuvre de Proust comprend ... une partie de doctrine—sur la finalité de l'art, sur la nature de la réalité, sur le moyen de réaliser l'Être total, de posséder l'Absolu—partie nettement mystique, par laquelle il se sépare radicalement de la tradition française, et ressortit en droiture au romantisme allemand. [55]

An American, Stuart Atkins, likewise suggests the affinity with the German: "At a time when the French novel is for the first time generally longer than the German, when an almost Germanic spirit of metaphysical disquietude is a striking characteristic of much French writing." [56]

### Nature and objectives of literature

It is self-evident that in a period in which the word poetry obtains such vague and lofty connotation, the distinctions of Monsieur Jourdain exist no longer. If poetry means essentially a spiritual exercise, prose has been relegated to the mere communication of ideas. And poetry, in the process of its transformation and transfiguration, has been divested of most of its conventional attributes. There is little question of prosody. Syntax is reduced to a few simple liaisons by which free association of images may be connected. If poetry is pure spontaneity, why mount it on an armature of logic and reason? Matters of form, technique, *métier* are

---

[49] Manifestoes in *Fontaine* (March, 1943).
[50] Raymond, *op. cit.,* p. 130.
[51] *Ibid.,* pp. 173–74.
[52] Apollinaire, "L'Esprit nouveau et les poètes," *Mercure de France,* December 1, 1918, p. 392.
[53] Preface to G. Chennevière, *Oeuvres poétiques* (Gallimard, 1929).
[54] Béguin, *L'Ame romantique et le rêve,* pp. 400–401.
[55] Benda, *op. cit.,* p. 205.
[56] *Yale French Studies,* VI, 43.

incompatible with poetry's essential nature. Whatever the genre—novel, theater, essay, verse—the vision must be preserved as closely as possible to its original state. To polish style, chisel sonnets appear trivial and tiresome games which lead an artist far from his mission. A work of art is a sort of by-product to an artistic life. As Giraudoux said of Rimbaud that writing is an accident in the life of a poet, Camus declares that art cannot be the end, the meaning, and the consolation of a life. "Le grand artiste ... est avant tout un grand vivant." Camus, too, has Rimbaud in mind, for he adds, "Le créateur ... ne tient pas à son oeuvre. Il pourrait y renoncer. Il y renonce quelquefois. Il suffit d'une Abyssinie." [57] We may consider the modern attitude diametrically opposed to everything Flaubert preached: form, perfection, Art.

But while it is perfectly clear that the contemporary writers reject the notion of the *poeta fabricans,* it is inexact to identify poetry exactly with the welter of the unconscious. Apollinaire's complete surrender to inspiration while creating does not mean that he did not direct and later consciously alter his reveries. Some intellectual collaboration is readily admitted. Even the Surrealists recognized that a poem was not the same thing as a dream. The famous debates over *poésie pure* have threshed out the interesting question of the unconscious element in a work of art. Partisans of *poésie pure* maintained that combinations of words take on values apart from their specific meaning and produce a pleasure which has nothing to do with comprehension, sympathy, appreciation of the justness or ingeniousness of the expression.[58] Henri Bremond and his followers found the essence of poetry in the *pouvoir encantatoire* described by Rimbaud, Baudelaire, and the Germans. Whereas they attributed all to inspiration, Valéry insisted upon the intellectual collaboration required of any work of art. The matter seems settled, since Bremond finally agreed that *poésie pure* could hardly exist alone. Both camps considered narration, didactism, eloquence, etc., as impurities in poetry: "Réduire la poésie aux démarches de la connaissance rationnelle, du discours, c'est aller contre la nature même, c'st vouloir un cercle carré." [59] But Valéry's insistence upon the intellectual element which is introduced as the poetic vision is actually recorded, reflects the consensus of poetic theory in France. "Celui même qui veut écrire son rêve se doit d'être infiniment éveillé." [60] Many misunderstandings have arisen over this matter. It is incorrect to assume that even the most fervent defenders of the dream in literature do not admit conscious activity. We have observed that such a notion of Surrealistic doctrine is inexact. The Surrealists themselves appear to have misunderstood the German Romantics, for they too described the poet as the dreamer awake. Rousseaux, remarking upon Béguin's *L'Ame romantique et le rêve,* points out that the mysteries of the dream have always been implicit in poetry. But the German Romantics were the first to put "le mystère en pleine lumière." [61]

[57] *Op. cit.,* 134 (see pages 21 and 97 of present work).
[58] In this connection one should remember Tieck and Hoffmann's experiments with language as music.
[59] Bremond, *La Poésie pure* (Grasset, 1926), p. 16.
[60] *Variété I* (Gallimard, 1924), p. 56.
[61] Rousseaux, *op. cit.,* p. 214.

The modern conception, in line with Novalis' definition, implies a fusion, or better, a lack of distinction between rational and irrational elements. It looks back to a primitive age before man's faculties were divided, when poetry was an integral expression of man. We have noticed the myth of primitive man in connection with the *Märchen* and with Giraudoux and the Surrealists. The Cubists can probably be considered its inventors in our century. They perceived in the Negro art which was all in fashion about 1907 elements which sophisticated art had buried under layers of civilization. By extolling such a coarse genius as Jarry and such a naïve genius as Rousseau they established the ideal of primitivism which still prevails. In his verses André Spire aspires to the power and authenticity of the "cri émotionnel du langage non encore articulé par lequel l'homme primitif agissait sur autrui comme un organe sur un organe." [62] Claudel's rejection of prosody is based on grounds similar to those of Grimm's primitivism. Contemporary poets follow the German thesis that poetry was purest and greatest in the Golden Age of naïve man, before artifice and judgment corrupted it. Although Proust could not bring himself to accept as a doctrine that first drafts are superior to subsequent correction, could not go so far as Tieck or Giraudoux, he suggests timidly in a letter to Jacques Emile Blanche that "il peut se faire qu'un premier jet ait une sève que des corrections trop restrictives arrêteront." [63]

Primitivism is an expression of the contemporary "furie du total," to use Benda's phrase. Before the development of hierarchized knowledge or perception, man could embrace the world in its totality. Paul Claudel ecstatically announces that we still may: "Ouvrez les yeux! Le monde est encore intact, il est vierge comme au premier jour, frais comme le lait ... l'univers est total! Salut donc, ô monde nouveau à mes yeux, ô monde maintenant total!" [64] Such affirmations of totality have for some Frenchmen a very German sound. Boutroux claimed it is characteristically German to conceive of things under the category of all, whereas French under the category of the one. Benda charges the Prousts, Gides, Claudels, and their flocks of deserting the French and going over to the German side: "Chose qui nous semble indéniable, pour autant que l'on croie à la *Völkerpsychologie*." [65] He might well have mentioned Apollinaire as first to migrate. Apollinaire, who before Giraudoux had sojourned in Germany, counseled art and literature to try to grasp all things in their totality, "exalter la vie sous quelque forme qu'elle se présente." [66] Certainly the leading spirits of our period have seemed bent upon abolishing distinctions on all fronts. Boutroux and Bergson rejoin Schlegel and Novalis in denying the distinctions between philosophy and art. Bergson wrote that Ravaisson's entire philosophy derives from the idea that art is figurative metaphysics, that metaphysics is a reflection upon art, and that it is the same intuition, diversely utilized,

---

[62] Raymond, *op. cit.*, p. 211.

[63] Marcel Proust, *Correspondance générale* (Plon, 1932), III, 139.

[64] Paul Claudel, *Art poétique*. (Text reproduced in Pierre Angers, *Commentaire à l'Art poétique*, Mercure de France, 1949, pp. 93–95.)

[65] Benda, *op. cit.*, p. 57. [The philosophy of these writers is contained in the words of Hegel: "Das Wahre ist das Ganze" (cited by Benda, p. 55).]

[66] Apollinaire, "L'Esprit nouveau et les poètes," *Mercure de France*, December 1, 1918, p. 385.

which makes the profound philosopher and the great artist.[67] Their point of view
is endorsed by Albert Camus who declares: "On ne saurait trop insister sur
l'arbitraire de l'ancienne opposition entre art et philosophie" and is borne out by all
our artist philosophers like Proust, Gide, Valéry, Claudel, and Sartre.[68] Proust in
Le Temps retrouvé hopes to suppress the line separating present and past. Gide, in
the field of morality, refuses to see evil as the counterpart of virtue. Most recently
Sartre voices the same desire. As a consequence of his totalitarian philosophy, Sartre
conceives of the myth as the most suitable literary vehicle because it alone can embrace the whole. Not long ago in this country he announced his disapproval of
naturalism, "tranches de vie," for its superficiality and incompleteness. Schlegel
and Schelling had, we remember, proposed the myth to the German Romantic
poets. Another aspect of this trend toward unification may be observed in the recent vogue of pantheistic notions, which Benda traces to the Germans. There are
many among recent writers who seem to admit no differentiation between God and
the World. And the individual consciousness is identified with the universal: "Le
drame universel et le drame humain tendent à s'égaler." The modern attitude is
summed up by Albert Thibaudet in the following words: "Ces idées de droite et de
gauche sont des coupes arbitraires de concepts sur une réalité mouvante et
complexe." [69]

In the work itself the prejudice against classification and limitation is everywhere apparent. "Das Vorrecht der Kunst ist Einheit." [70] Bergson had advanced
the notion that melody is the type of artistic realization par excellence because it
flows on without clearly defined succession. The whole trend is toward blending
and fusion. Synaesthesia which we can observe in Tieck already before Baudelaire
is now widely exploited. "Die Farbe klingt, / die Form ertönt, jedwede / hat nach
der Form und Farbe Zung und Rede . . . / Sich Farbe, Duft, Gesang Geschwister
nennen." [71] Confusion of genres, general formlessness, mingling of the arts have
literally achieved the German ideal of the Gesamtkunstwerk. One of the most
interesting manifestations is the desire of writers to achieve an effect of simultaneity
in their writings. Proust deplored that literature cannot present things as in pic-
torial art. Benda compares his attitude with that of Hegel, who opposed the
instantaneousness of the effect caused by the plastic arts with the succession which
literature implies. But the cubist poets tried to accomplish precisely the effect of
plastic arts. Apollinaire and Pierre Reverdy tried to suggest the totality of an object
instead of showing just one side. Claudel stresses simultaneity in the artistic conception: "Je ne suis pas un homme qui pense par succession, je pense toute une

[67] Bergson, "La Vie et l'Oeuvre de Ravaisson," La Pensée et le Mouvement (Geneva: Skira,
1945).
[68] Op. cit., p. 133.
[69] "Réflexions," La Nouvelle Revue française, July 1, 1934, p. 93.
[70] F. Schlegel, Über das Studium der griechischen Poesie. (Cited by Helene Baader, "Organische
Kunstauffassung im modernen Frankreich," Germanisch-Romanische Monatsschrift, XVI (1928),
322.)
[71] Tieck, Zerbino (cited by Brandes, op. cit., p. 41).

oeuvre à la fois, et jamais une partie ne se développe sans qu'elle sente sur elle le consentement ou la gêne des autres parties."[72]

To restore the primitive vision, to suggest the totality of things, contemporary poets have renounced all other attributes of their art to concentrate upon the metaphor. In their hands there can be no more question of the metaphor being a vain ornament of rhetoric, "a jewel sewn upon the stout fabric of a narrative."[73] It is the basic stuff of which literature is made. Jean de Pierrefeu notes its role in modern literature: "La métaphore ... il y aurait tout un chapitre à écrire sur la transformation de cette figure de rhétorique qui de simple ornement de la phrase est devenue, chez les modernes, presque toute la phrase."[74] They invest it with all the properties of an epistemological instrument, a means of apprehending the highest reality. Through its manipulation the secret organization of nature can be at last exposed to these indefatigable seekers after the absolute. The primitive order is re-established and the Romantic dream is fulfilled. Through poetic magic the walls which the *raison raisonnante* has erected tumble; its pattern and hierarchy dissolve before the hidden affinities which the poet brings to light. "Le réel occulte, que le voile des apparences—des perceptions normales, des sentiments trop vite définissables, des idées claires—nous masque, ce réel occulte c'est aux images qu'il appartient de le dénuder dans un éclair, de le rendre sensible au coeur."[75]

It goes without saying that the sacred metaphor should not be confused with any intellectually engendered conceit. The Romantic doctrine of the poet's passiveness, the spontaneity of his creation, is here in full force. The metaphor is a revelation. Marcel Proust, who states eloquently the point of view of the tradition developing since Symbolism, insists upon the mysterious "inevitability" of the metaphor. He cannot tolerate any comparison which is not imperative. Only when the poet grasps the *rapport unique* which unites two disparate objects can he expose their inner nature, their essence, and they are then removed from the contingencies of time and space. Symbolist poets, from Baudelaire to Claudel, have made the inevitable metaphor the fetish of their lyric incantations. Through Baudelaire, speaking of Gautier, we hear the teachings of the German mystics:

Si l'on réfléchit qu'à cette merveilleuse faculté (for using the exact word) Gautier unit une immense intelligence innée de la *correspondance* et du symbolisme universels, ce répertoire de toute métaphore, on comprendra qu'il puisse sans cesse, sans fatigue comme sans faute, définir l'attitude mystérieuse que les objets de la création tiennent devant le regard de l'homme. Il y a dans le mot, dans le *verbe,* quelque chose de *sacré* qui nous défend d'en faire un jeu de hasard. Manier savamment une langue, c'est pratiquer une espèce de sorcellerie évocatoire.[76]

Paul Claudel echoes the same idea: "La métaphore, l'iambe fondamental ou rapport d'une grave et d'une aiguë, ne se joue pas qu'aux feuilles de nos livres: elle

[72] Jacques Rivière and Paul Claudel, *Correspondance 1907–14* (Plon-Nourrit, 1926), p. 10.
[73] J. Middleton Murry, *The Problem of Style* (London: Oxford University Press, 1922), p. 12.
[74] J. Pierrefeu, *Les Beaux Livres de notre temps* (Plon, 1938), p. 35.
[75] Raymond, *op. cit.,* p. 130.
[76] *Oeuvres complètes*, III, 164–65.

est l'art autochthone employé par tout ce qui naît. Et ne parlez pas de hasard." [77]

Many others have joined Proust in the conviction that the metaphor, as the supreme poetic device, is a key to the analogies which bind the universe. Paul Eluard voices the general attitude in affirming that "tout est comparable à tout, tout trouve son echo, sa raison, sa ressemblance, son opposition, son devenir partout." [78] Claudel, who will be satisfied with nothing short of total comprehension, total feeling, total possession, makes fundamental in his poetics the unity of the world and the correspondence of all nature. It is the artist's business to testify to this unity. "Par moi aucune chose ne reste plus seule mais je l'associe à une autre dans mon coeur." [79] Jean Cassou describes what the poetic image has come to mean:

Alors la poésie tente de réaliser une manifestation du monde purement qualitative. Elle se glisse dans les choses, leurs reflets, leurs déformations, leurs correspondances, leurs analogies. Les choses, non plus seulement les mots, mais les choses elles-mêmes, substantiellement, se voient arrachées à leur usage commun. L'image a été définie par Pierre Gueguen "une forme magique du principe d'identité." Dans chaque image, ce théologien esthétique voit une réconcentration de l'unité cosmique, une vision béatifique. [80]

Poetry has become the forest of symbols, analogies, which the Germans foresaw.

It has been a frequent reproach made to the German Romanticists that in spite of the fecundity of their theories, their own creative efforts are disappointing. One looks in vain for concrete expression of some of their teachings. Such seems to be the case in the matter of the metaphor. Contemporary writers far surpass in practice any Romantic attempt, even that of Jean Paul. New and foreign writers have developed and fulfilled the German esthetic ideas beyond their own timid efforts. The prestige and the supreme validity which the metaphor has come to assume in the twentieth century is an example of such fulfillment of Romantic theory.

The "soif de communion à la conscience universelle" [81] has led the high priests of contemporary French letters to regard themselves as occupying a position vis-à-vis their work analogous to that of the Creator of the world. The two creations become as one as the poet's work reflects and echoes the universe:

La connaissance des moyens dont dispose le poète nous a permis de concevoir son art comme la mise en oeuvre de puissances d'une nature identique à celles dont la Conscience universelle dispose dans ses jeux de création et de destruction. A ce point que le poète est en mesure de prévoir les développements de l'oeuvre divine, et d'en réaliser à l'avance dans ses poèmes le total épanouissement. Le mythe que le poète construit est à l'image de l'univers, et en contient les secrets. Le mythe reflète la conscience du poète comme l'univers celle de son auteur. ... Il nous apparaît que l'expérience poétique constitue pour l'homme un moyen de reconciliation avec l'univers, en même temps qu'une méthode de connaissance à la faveur de laquelle le mystère des choses devient leur vérité. [82]

[77] Claudel, *Art poétique* (*op. cit.*, p. 144).
[78] Eluard, *Donner à voir*, p. 134.
[79] Claudel, "L'Esprit et l'Eau," *Cinq Grandes Odes* (Gallimard, 1919), p. 52.
[80] Cassou, *Pour la poésie*, p. 28.
[81] Benda, *op. cit.*, p. 57.
[82] Rolland de Renéville. (Cited by Benda, *op. cit.*, p. 58.)

Claudel declares he takes from God his "esprit de Création." [83] Many others before him had hit upon the same idea. Particularly Schiller, who formulated it for the early Romantics. Albert Camus seems very close to Schiller when he recommends that the creator stand aloof from his work: "Le créateur absurde ne tient pas à son oeuvre. Il pourrait y renoncer." [84]

We have seen in the examples of the Romantic spirit which we have scrutinized most closely that mysticism is not the only means of refuting the positivistic or rational universe. German poets and modern Frenchmen have found liberation through humor. Apollinaire and all the fantasists such as Toulet, Jarry, Jacob, Cocteau oscillate between the two poles of emotion and sarcasm. Essentially mystics and idealists, they cultivate the *merveilleux* and the fanciful to discredit and escape from everyday reality. They could offer the "sacrificed generations" an escape from the odious realities caused by war. It is significant that Hoffmann enjoyed a great vogue during the between-wars period. Incidentally it is he who had so profoundly influenced Max Jacob as a child. Fargue, Supervielle, Alain-Fournier could also be studied as representative of this group of French writers who use all the tricks of the German humorists, including the *Stimmungsbrechung* which we have discussed in connection with Giraudoux. The sentiment of chaos, which the Germans hoped to attain through this device, appears to be exactly what we know today as the sentiment of the absurd. Albert Camus has built upon it a philosophy.

Yet French critics maintain that these descendants of Jules Laforgue never went so far as the German Romantics. They did not break so definitively with daily reality, but in Raymond's words, just lengthened the rope a little. He says, "Gardons-nous d'assimiler cette ironie à celle des romantiques allemands. Elle ne les mène pas jusqu'à ces hauteurs où, dépris de soi et de la réalité sensible, on ne perçoit plus rien que transfiguré, idéalisé." [85] One would say that this rope is a very slender and tenuous one in many cases. But if it is perfectly accurate that even as drastic a modern school as Surrealism hesitated before cutting all ties with common-sense reality, the same assertion could be made for the Germans. Their grip on reality was much stronger than the French seem inclined to think.

### Justification of the Present Essay

In examining, as we have done, dominant tendencies in contemporary French literary theory and practice in reference to the German school, the difficulties are many and obvious. The vastness and complexity of the subject precludes any pretence to completeness in this brief treatment. And the author's insufficiencies in such an undertaking would be felt by no one more keenly than himself. The dangers involved in trying to determine movements and attitudes among writers of one's own times or those whose last word has not been said are generally recog-

---

[83] Raymond, *op. cit.*, p. 130.
[84] *Op. cit.*, p. 134 (see p. 26 of present work).
[85] Raymond, *op. cit.*, p. 139.

nized. One wonders, however, if it is any easier to interpret more correctly a foreign and remote literary school deformed and blurred through successive generations. In pointing out affinities, understanding correctly an older literary program is a task as great as that involving a modern. Yet in spite of the inherent dangers and difficulties of the subject, I have felt that reference to the German Romantics would help clarify the picture of recent literature and help us place it in the long gallery of western art. The general disfavor of "source" studies in this country and nationalistic bias in France have for too long kept the German Romantic School from the place it deserves as initiators of modern literary theory. Before the testimony of the contemporary classics, we can no longer dismiss the problem of Franco-German literary relations after the manner of Pierre Lasserre:

Il est une autre sorte d'influence qu'il n'y a point lieu d'exclure de notre étude, parce que l'Allemagne est le seul pays d'Europe d'où nous ne l'ayons jamais reçue. C'est l'influence littéraire, je veux dire celle qui s'exerce sur les formes et les sujets de l'art littéraire, qui, de la part de l'antiquité au xviᵉ siècle, de l'antiquité, de l'Espagne et de l'Italie au xviiᵉ, de l'Angleterre au xviiiᵉ, de l'Angleterre encore au xixᵉ, et récemment de la Russie et des pays scandinaves, a été diversement heureuse, mais toujours si féconde pour la France. D'Allemagne, en ce genre, rien ou si peu que rien; quelques imitations lyriques de Schiller, de Bürger ou de Uhland, le bonnet fourré et le cabinet gothique du docteur Faust, mais non pas son esprit; quelques emprunts, en un mot, d'un petit pittoresque; rien en tout cas de général, aucun «mouvement.»[86]

[86] Lasserre, *op. cit.*, p. 473.